CW00925573

The Spokesman

Genocide Old and New

Edited by Ken Coates

Published by Spokesman for the Bertrand Russell Peace Foundation

Spokesman 93   2007

CONTENTS

Cover photo: The entrance to Auschwitz

Printed by the Russell Press Ltd., Nottingham, UK

ISSN 0262 7922

ISBN 0 85124 733 4

Subscriptions
Institutions £35.00
Individuals £20.00 (UK)
        £25.00 (ex UK)

Back issues available on request

A CIP catalogue record for this book is available from the British Library

Published by the
Bertrand Russell Peace Foundation Ltd.,
Russell House
Bulwell Lane
Nottingham NG6 0BT
England
Tel. 0115 9784504
email:
elfeuro@compuserve.com
www.spokesmanbooks.com
www.russfound.org

Editorial

Genocide Old and New

The mid-term Congressional Elections in the United States gave a clear majority to the Democrats in the House of Representatives. They even gave the Democrats a narrow victory in the Election for the Senate. Of course, the Democrats reflect a variety of views on the war in Iraq: but whatever their own views, it was quite impossible to see their triumph as anything rather than a repudiation of the policies of President George W. Bush. As if to confirm this judgement, Defence Secretary Donald Rumsfeld instantly resigned. He was replaced by Robert Gates, a close intimate of the present President's father, President George H. W. Bush. His foreign policy team diverged in many respects from the current President's policy.

Mr. Gates was already a member of the Iraq Study Group, which was led by a colleague of his, James Baker, former Secretary of State. It involved a number of leading old-school Republicans and senior Democrats. It was widely expected that the ISG would ultimately argue for direct talks between the United States and Iran, as the other preponderant influence over events in Iraq. If clues were sought about the outcome of this report, it would be hard to find them in the statements of the British Prime Minister. Certainly he was voluble as ever after the defeat of his American allies. But he still proclaimed the need for co-operation in their efforts in shrill and peremptory tones, clothing his peace initiative towards Iran and Syria (if such it was) in the language of near-hysterical denunciation.

Of course, the neo-cons, both in their American and British incarnations, have boxed themselves into an impossibly uncomfortable corner. They insist that the Iranians furnish a core component of the axis of evil, whilst at the same time proclaiming, with no evidence whatever, that they are simultaneously hell-bent on the acquisition of nuclear weapons.

It is very difficult to maintain these views with the requisite degree of stridency whilst calling upon your adversaries to initiate a major new peace initiative. All the time, in the background, is the insistent report of military preparations. Colonel Gardiner, who had been commissioned to identify Iranian installations for targeting for possible bombardment, made a blunt report of his activities shortly before the mid-term Elections.[1]

For some years there had been concern about the confrontation between the United States and Iran. This has continuously given rise to apprehension, as leaks from the American Intelligence Services, and the notable dispatches of Seymour Hersh, have raised alarm from time to time.

But there have been other voices which, without being sanguine, have been somewhat more reassuring. Discounting the apologists for the American administration, there have been serious voices from the United States Intelligence, and the American military, explaining why the military and social costs of an extension of the Middle East war to Iran would be prohibitive, wreaking far more damage on American interests than it would be rational to risk. This view has not usually been founded on any moral rejection of the awful consequences of war, but on calculations of its likely consequences.

Quite generally this nowadays excludes the possibility of any ground offensive. What has been a more open question has been whether the United States might launch air attacks.

The remarkable story of the offensive against Lebanon, which suffered prolonged Israeli bombardment and immense destruction, and yet remained undefeated, would have given serious thought to military planners in the United States. It certainly seems that the opposition of the British and American Governments to an immediate ceasefire in Lebanon was based on the calculation that, given sufficient time, the Israelis would be able to destroy Hezbollah, even if this process involved the most widespread material destruction, and very large numbers of civilian casualties. But Hezbollah was not crushed, and indeed, according to its leader Sayed Hassan Nasrallah, it emerged from that terrible conflict stronger in popular support, and indeed, even in a stronger military position than it held at the beginning.

But there have been insistent noises from the Bush entourage, not only accusing Hezbollah of being proxies for Iran, but also threatening to visit a similar destruction upon Iran from the air, like that which has afflicted the Lebanon. As sometimes happens, events that might provide an awesome deterrent to rational people may sometimes be an incentive to military adventurism.

At this point we received the report from Sam Gardiner. He thinks that the consequences of a serious air strike on Iran can be incalculable. But he thinks that whereas military rationality might have prevailed heretofore, today the issue is perilously more uncertain.

His conclusion is very chilling. Just prior to any anticipated strike, he says we can expect the quiet deployment of Air Force tankers to staging bases, and 'we will see additional Navy assets moved to the region'. There will also be a fierce intensification of the propaganda preparations for war on terrorism.

All of us are well aware of some of the recent propaganda moves in this direction. Now, more ominously, a significant 'Strike Group' of ships has arrived in the Persian Gulf. On September 21st it was reported in *The Nation* that:

'the Eisenhower Strike Group bristling with Tomahawk cruise missiles, has received orders to depart the United States in a little over a week ... other official sources ... confirm that this armada is scheduled to arrive off the coast of Iran on or around October 21st.'

Even after the Elections, Seymour Hersh reiterated his views that the White House feared that the victorious Democrats might prohibit the financing of operations aimed at overthrowing or destabilising the Iranian Government, to prevent it from acquiring the bomb.

'They are afraid that Congress is going to vote a binding resolution to stop a hit on Iran, à la Nicaragua in the Contra war.'

Hersh recalled that in late 1982 Edward P. Boland, a Democrat, introduced the first of his amendments which restricted the Reagan administration's ability to support the Contras, who were actively seeking the overthrow of the Sandinista Government in Nicaragua. This led directly to the White House initiating the clandestine sale of American weaponry, via Israel, to Iran, in order to raise covert funds for onward transmission to the Contras in Nicaragua. All this, said Hersh, was recollected by Vice President Cheney shortly before the mid-term Elections, when he claimed in a conversation (of which he now says he has no record) that whatever Congress under new management might say, the Bush administration would be able to find ways to circumvent it. So we came to hear a new mantra: 'We are not looking for an exit strategy. We are looking for victory.'

So it comes about that the alliance recruits a powerful new task force of Leprechauns, and all stride forth armed with shovels, to the end of the rainbow where victory is to be found in a pot of gold. Or maybe not ...

But for now, we must continue to try to decode the barrage of contradictory messages which come from officialdom. Perhaps the most interesting of these is to be found in the report of the Task Force established by the Council on Foreign Relations, under the co-chairmanship of the same Robert M. Gates, and President Carter's former adviser, Zbig Brzezinski. This has the encouraging title: *Iran: Time for a New Approach.*[2]

Their Task Force reasserts the uncertainty of its members about the precise nature of the Iranian Government's policy on the development of nuclear weapons. But,

'at the core of the Task Force's conclusions is the recognition that it is in the interests of the United States to engage selectively with Iran to promote regional stability, dissuade Iran from pursuing nuclear weapons, preserve reliable energy supplies, reduce the threat of terror, and address the "democracy deficit" that pervades the Middle East as a whole. For these reasons, the members advocate a revised strategic approach to Iran.

A Revised Approach to Iran
The Task Force concludes that the current lack of sustained engagement with Iran harms US interests in a critical region of the world and that direct dialogue with Tehran on specific areas of mutual concern should be pursued.

1. A political dialogue with Iran should not be deferred until such a time as the deep differences over Iranian nuclear ambitions and its invidious involvement with regional conflicts have been resolved. Rather, the process of selective political engagement itself represents a potentially effective path for addressing those differences. Just as the United States maintains a constructive relationship with China (and earlier did so with the Soviet Union) while strongly opposing certain aspects of its internal and international policies, Washington should approach Iran with a readiness to explore areas of common interests, while continuing to contest objectionable policies. Ultimately, any real rapprochement with Tehran can only occur in the context of meaningful progress on the most urgent US concerns surrounding nuclear weapons, terrorism, and regional stability.

2. A "grand bargain" that would settle comprehensively the outstanding conflicts between Iran and the United States is not a realistic goal, and pursuing such an outcome would be unlikely to produce near-term progress on Washington's central interests. Instead, the Task Force proposes selectively engaging Iran on issues where US and Iranian interests converge, and building upon incremental progress to tackle the broader range of concerns that divide the two governments.

3. US policies towards Tehran should make use of incentives as well as punitive measures. The US reliance on comprehensive, unilateral sanctions has not succeeded in its stated objective to alter Iranian conduct and has deprived Washington of greater leverage vis-à-vis the Iranian government apart from the threat of force. Given the increasingly important role of economic interests in shaping Iran's policy options at home and abroad, the prospect of commercial relations with the United States could be a powerful tool in Washington's arsenal.

4. The United States should advocate democracy in Iran without relying on the rhetoric of regime change, as that would be likely to arouse nationalist sentiments in defense of the current regime even among those who currently oppose it. The US government should focus its rhetoric and its policies on promoting political evolution that encourages Iran to develop stronger democratic institutions at home and enhanced diplomatic and economic relations abroad. Engaging with the current government to address pressing regional and international issues need not contradict US support for these objectives; indeed, engagement pursued judiciously would enhance the chances of internal change in Iran.

5. The Task Force is mindful of repeated efforts over the last twenty-five years to engage the regime in Tehran, and that all of these have come to naught for various reasons. However, the Task Force believes that the US military intervention along Iran's flanks in both Afghanistan and Iraq has changed the geopolitical landscape in the region. These changes may offer both the United States and Iran new incentives to open a mutually beneficial dialogue, first on issues of common interest, such as regional stability, and eventually on the tough issues of terrorism and proliferation. We recognize that even the most perspicacious policy toward Iran may be stymied by Iranian obstinacy.'

Apparently we live in an age in which the world's major megapower has evolved not one but a plurality of foreign policies, alongside their military concomitants. At such a time it is more than ever urgent that the task of watching over these sombre developments be undertaken by a large and resourceful peace movement. It is also more important than ever that the peoples of the world should resist the concentration of far more fearful weapons of mass destruction in the hands of such unstable, indeed volatile powers.

* * *

When last the Polaris nuclear system was upgraded in Britain, the decision was virtually clandestine. Although it was to prove most costly, when the true story was revealed under the Thatcher administration, it caused an unholy row in the Labour Party, which, at the end of the seventies, had been told nothing, or nearly nothing, about it. Now John Reid has tried to make a great virtue of what he pretends is 'greater openness'. True, there will be some sort of a vote, about something, in the House of Commons. What exactly it will entail is still, however, shrouded in mystery. What seems clear is that the new Trident programme will be scheduled to continue over several decades, and to involve prodigious continuing expenditure. It seems equally likely that the Government will seek to build in a variety of failsafe mechanisms, to prevent a more humane or rational administration from altering the programme.

Obviously the Americans will have a powerful influence on all this. The wholly subservient 'British' deterrent is pretty much the most significant material remnant of the special relationship between Britain and the United States, but the current administration will undoubtedly see it as part of the contract which was accepted when Tony Blair signed up for George Bush's Iraq war.

There are two snags about confirming the deployment of this renewed programme to create weapons of mass destruction.

Firstly, there will be a Parliamentary vote to give its approval in some form or other. This may not amount to overmuch, but it will at least afford the citizens an opportunity to vote against every one of their representatives who has given support to the new generation of nukes. Within the prevailing state of political alienation, many heads should roll. The big Parties in Parliament may well become smaller, as a result. The small Parties, where conscience may survive, may equally well increase. Few will doubt that this process will be good for British morals, not to say morale. But second, this particular vote may give rise to a qualitatively new constitutional development.

Below we publish statements by two most distinguished Church leaders in Scotland. Both are firmly opposed to the new Trident programme, which impacts with especial force on Scotland.

The so-called British deterrent is now situated solely in Scotland, and the weapons which were formerly deployed in England have all been dismantled since the late years of the last century. Scots are increasingly aware of the dangers involved in the nuclear facilities at Faslane. The clones will heartily insist that the Scottish deployment of weapons of mass destruction is a direct response to the defence needs of the United Kingdom. But the electorate may take a dim view of this commitment, since it offers no benefits to Scotland. Indeed, there could be few more telling arguments in favour of Scottish independence than this: that it offers the most secure road to Scottish disengagement from Mr. Blair's poisonous wars, and from his illegal weapons. Mr. Blair's shrill nuclear patriotism may bring about the implosion of more than the allegedly British WMD. It might also terminate the United Kingdom, and thus the Labour Party. If Scotland secedes, then unless something very radical in the English polity develops, very quickly, the conservative instincts of the English will determine the composition of the English Parliament.

All in all, the temptation of nuclear defence could quite possibly remove that which was supposed to be defended. Will anybody think of this in time?

*   *   *

We are honoured once again to be able to publish the incomparable Robert Fisk in this number of *The Spokesman*.

'The First Holocaust' is a chapter from his book on *The Great War for Civilisation: The Conquest of the Middle East*. This represents a vast labour, and, he tells us, was sixteen years in the making. It has consumed 1,368 pages, and earned great praises on all sides. Its literary quality needs no commendation from us. But why have we chosen a chapter on the Armenian genocide to represent this great book here, when it is also alive with reports of contemporary traumas, in Afghanistan or Lebanon, Iraq, Iran or Algeria?

There have been, in short, innumerable cruelties in the conquest of the Middle East, but in one sense the most shocking thing about these often criminal acts is that the screams of their victims have so frequently gone unheard. The great warriors who have sought to impose their own mean civilisation on peoples whose culture is as old as time, have also imposed selective hearing, discriminate memory. A celebration of happy indifference.

Fisk has unerringly homed in on the Armenian massacres as a classic symbol of these responses. With his help, we can try to count the dead. But far more significantly, we can begin to understand the vital necessity of memory in defending the humanity of its victims. Because of its length, we have divided this piece into two parts, the first of which appears below. The second will follow.

Ken Coates

Footnote:
1. *The End of the 'Summer of Diplomacy': Assessing US Military Options in Iran*, Sam Gardiner, USAF (Ret.), The Century Foundation, September 2006.
2. *Iran: Time for a New Approach*, Report of an Independent Task Force sponsored by the Council on Foreign Relations. Zbigniew Brzezinski and Robert M. Gates, Co-Chairs, Suzanne Maloney, Project Director, July 2004.

Genocide

Raphael Lemkin

Professor Lemkin was born in Poland in 1900 and died in the United States in 1959. In 1944, in his book Axis Rule in Occupied Europe, *Lemkin analysed the laws of the Nazi Reich and showed they were intended to facilitate the destruction of whole populations. Lemkin coined a word for this – genocide. Following the creation of the United Nations, he worked to establish the 1946 Declaration and the 1948 Convention on Genocide and have them adopted by the General Assembly. This excerpt is taken from Professor Lemkin's essay 'Genocide' which he published in 1946.*

The last war has focused our attention on the phenomenon of the destruction of whole populations – of national, racial and religious groups – both biologically and culturally. The German practices, especially in the course of occupation, are too well known. Their general plan was to win the peace though the war be lost, and that goal could have been achieved through successfully changing the political and demographic interrelationships in Europe in favour of Germany. The population not destroyed was to be integrated in the German cultural, political and economic pattern.

In this way a mass obliteration of nationhoods had been planned throughout occupied Europe. The Nazi leaders had stated very bluntly their intent to wipe out the Poles, the Russians; to destroy demographically and culturally the French element in Alsace-Lorraine, the Slavonians in Carniola and Carinthia. They almost achieved their goal in exterminating the Jews and Gypsies in Europe. Obviously, the German experience is the most striking and the most deliberate and thorough, but history has provided us with other examples of the destruction of entire nations, and ethnic and religious groups. There are, for example, the destruction of Carthage; that of religious groups in the wars of Islam and the Crusades; the massacres of the Albigenses and the Waldenses; and more recently, the massacre of the Armenians.

While society sought protection against individual crimes, or rather crimes directed against individuals, there has been no serious endeavour hitherto to prevent and punish the murder and destruction of millions. Apparently, there was not even an adequate name for such a phenomenon. Referring to the Nazi butchery in the present war, Winston Churchill said in his broadcast of August, 1941, 'We are in the presence of a crime without a name'.

The word 'genocide'

Would mass murder be an adequate name for

such a phenomenon? We think not, since it does not connote the motivation of the crime, especially when the motivation is based upon racial, national or religious considerations. An attempt to destroy a nation and obliterate its cultural personality was hitherto called denationalisation. This term seems to be inadequate, since it does not connote biological destruction. On the other hand, this term is mostly used for conveying or for defining an act of deprivation of citizenship. Many authors, instead of using a generic term, use terms connoting only some functional aspect of the main generic notion of the destruction of nations and races. Thus, the terms 'Germanisation', 'Italianisation', 'Magyarisation' are used often to connote the imposition by a stronger nation (Germany, Italy, Hungary) of its national pattern upon a group controlled by it. These terms are inadequate since they do not convey biological destruction, and they cannot be used as a generic term. In the case of Germany, it would be ridiculous to speak about the Germanisation of the Jews or Poles in western Poland, since the Germans wanted these groups eradicated entirely.

Hitler stated many times that Germanisation could only be carried out with the soil, never with men. These considerations led the author of this article to the necessity of coining a new term for this particular concept: genocide. This word is made from the ancient Greek word *genos* (race, clan) and the Latin suffix *cide* (killing). Thus, genocide in its formation would correspond to such words as tyrannicide, homicide, patricide ...

On Genocide

Jean-Paul Sartre

Jean-Paul Sartre presided over the International War Crimes Tribunal, founded by Bertrand Russell, in Stockholm in May 1967. Later that year, at the second session of the Tribunal in Roskilde in Denmark, he presented his report on genocide in Vietnam.

The word 'genocide' has not been in existence for very long: it was the jurist Lemkin who coined it between the two world wars. The *thing* itself is as old as humanity and there has never been a society whose structure has preserved it from committing this crime. All genocide is a product of history and it always carries the signs of the society from which it springs. The case which we have to judge concerns the largest contemporary capitalist power. It is as such that we must attempt to consider it; in other words, inasmuch as it expresses the economic structure, the political aims and the contradictions of that power.

In particular, we must try to understand whether there is an *intention of genocide* in the war that the American government is fighting against Vietnam. Article 2 of the Convention of 1948 defines genocide on the basis of intention. The Convention was tacitly referring to very recent history. Hitler had declared a deliberate plan to exterminate the Jews; he did not conceal the fact that he was using genocide as a *political tactic*. The Jew had to be put to death, wherever he came from, not because he had taken up arms or had joined a resistance movement, but just *because he was a Jew*. The American government, on the other hand, has made no such clear declarations. It even averred that it was going to the rescue of its allies, the South Vietnamese, who had been attacked by the Communists from the North. Is it possible for us, in objectively studying the facts, to unveil their hidden intention? And can we, after this examination, say that the armed forces of the USA are killing Vietnamese in Vietnam for the simple reason that they are Vietnamese?

This can only be established after a look at history: the structures of war change at the same time as those of society. From 1860 to this day, military motives and objectives have undergone a profound change and the end result of this metamorphosis is precisely the war of 'example' that the USA is waging in Vietnam.

1856: Treaties for the preservation of the property of neutrals;
1864: At Geneva, an attempt to protect the wounded;
1899, 1907: At The Hague, two Conferences attempting to control conflicts.

It is no coincidence if jurists and governments have multiplied agreements to 'humanise war' on the eve of two of the most horrifying massacres that man has ever known. Vladimir Dedijer has shown very well in his book *On Military Conventions* that capitalist societies were all simultaneously creating this monster, total war, which expresses their real nature. This is because:

1. Competition between the industrialised nations fighting over new markets engenders a permanent hostility which is expressed, both in theory and in practice, by what is called 'bourgeois nationalism'.

2. The development of industry, which is the source of these antagonisms, enables them to be resolved at the expense of one competitor, in the production of more and more *massively* lethal arms. The result of this evolution is that it becomes less and less possible to distinguish the rear from the front line, between the civilian population and the soldiers.

3. More military objectives appear, near to the cities. The *factories*, even if they are not working for the armies, do comprise the economic potential of a country. Therefore, the destruction of this potential becomes the aim of the war and the means by which it may be won.

4. For this reason, everybody is mobilised: the peasant fights at the front, the labourer is a soldier in the second line, the wives of the peasants replace the men in the fields. In the *total* effort of one country against another, the worker tends to become a fighter because, in the end, it is the strongest economic power that has the greatest chance of winning.

5. Finally, the democratic evolution of the bourgeois countries interests the masses in politics. The masses do not control the decisions of the state, but gradually gain a self-awareness. When a war comes, they no longer feel detached. Thus, reappraised and often deformed by propaganda, war becomes an ethical decision of the whole community. In every nation engaged in war manipulation makes all, or nearly all, the citizens the enemies of the other nation. In this way war becomes total.

6. These same technologically advanced societies do not cease to enlarge upon the field of competition in multiplying the means of communication. The well-known 'One World' of the Americans already existed at the end of the nineteenth century when the wheat from Argentina managed to ruin the farmers in Britain. War is total not only because all the members of one community are at war against the members of another, but because its risk embraces the whole world.

Therefore the war of bourgeois nations – of which the conflict of 1914 is the first example, but which had been menacing Europe since 1900 – is not the invention of one man or one government, but the simple necessity since the beginning of the century for a totalitarian effort against those who wish to carry on their politics by other means or methods. In other words, the option is clear; no war or total war. It was total war that our fathers fought. And the governments –

who could see it coming but did not have the intelligence or the courage to avoid it – tried vainly to humanise it.

However, in the First World War, intentions of genocide only appeared sporadically. The primary aim – as in the two centuries previously – was to destroy the military strength of a country, even if the more profound aim was to ruin its economy. But, although it was sometimes difficult to distinguish the civilians from the soldiers, it was rare, except during a few terroristic raids, for the population itself to be a target. Further, the two sides were developed nations, which implied from the outset a certain balance inasmuch as each side had a sufficient deterrent against the threat of extermination: the possibility for retaliation. This explains how, even in the midst of the massacre, a certain caution was observed.

However, since 1830 and throughout the last century, there have been many genocides outside Europe, some of which were the expression of authoritarian political structures, while the others – those which we need to know about to understand the growth of US imperialism and the nature of the war in Vietnam – found their origin in capitalistic democracies. To export goods and capital, the big powers, and in particular Great Britain and France, built themselves colonial empires. The name by which the French called their conquests – 'overseas possessions' – clearly indicates that they could only have acquired them by wars of aggression, seeking out the foe in his own country, in Africa, in Asia and in the underdeveloped lands. Far from being 'total wars', which would indicate a certain initial reciprocity, such complete superiority of arms only required an Expeditionary Force. This easily conquered any regular armies that existed, but because such barefaced aggression provoked the hatred of the civilian populations, which is the reserve of manpower or soldiers, the colonial troops imposed themselves by the terror of constant massacres. These massacres had all the characteristics of genocide: they involved destruction of 'one part of the group' (ethnic, national, religious) to terrorise the rest and break down the indigenous social structure. When the French had made a bloodbath of Algeria during the nineteenth century, they imposed on this tribal society – where every community possessed its own indivisible lands – the *Code Civile*, which consists of bourgeois jurisdiction with regard to the division of inherited property. Thus, they systematically destroyed the economic structure of the country. The land soon passed from the peasant tribes into the hands of merchants who had come from France. In fact, colonialisation is not just a simple conquest – as was the case in 1870 when Germany annexed Alsace-Lorraine – it is necessarily a cultural genocide. One cannot colonise without systematically destroying the particular character of the natives, at the same time denying them the right of integration with the mother country and of benefiting from its advantages. Colonialism is, in effect, a system: the colony sells raw materials and foodstuffs at a favourable price to the colonial power which then sells industrial goods back to them at world market prices. This peculiar method of exchange can only be established when the native labour is made to work for starvation wages. It naturally follows that the colonised lose their national personality, their culture, their customs, sometimes even their language, and live in misery like shadows constantly reminded of their own sub-humanity.

Yet their value as virtually free labour protects them to a certain extent from genocide. The Nuremberg Tribunal was fresh in the memory when the French, to make an example, massacred 45,000 Algerians at Sétif. This was such a common occurrence that no one then thought of judging the French government as the Nazis had been judged. But this deliberate destruction of 'one part of the national group' could not be continued without proving to the disadvantage of the settlers. To have done so would have ruined them. It is because they were unable to liquidate the Algerian population, and because they did not integrate the country, that the French lost the war in Algeria.

These comments enable us to understand how the nature of colonial wars was transformed after the Second World War. It is at about this period, in fact, that the people in the colonies, enlightened by such conflict and its impact on the 'empires', and encouraged by Mao Tse-tung's victory, determined to regain their national independence.

The characteristics of the struggle were clear from the beginning: the settlers were superior in arms, the colonised in numbers. Even in Algeria – a colony of settlers rather than of outside exploitation – the ratio of settlers to natives was 1:9. During the two world wars, many native peoples had learned the military arts and become well-seasoned soldiers. However, the scarcity and quality of weapons – at least at the beginning – limited the number of fighting units. These conditions dictated the nature of the fighting: terrorism, ambush, harassing the enemy, and the extreme mobility of the combat groups which had to strike unexpectedly and disappear immediately. This was not possible without the participation of the entire population. Hence the well-known association of the forces of liberation with the masses: the former organising agrarian reform, political bodies and education; the latter supporting, feeding and hiding the liberation army's soldiers, and giving them their young to replace their losses.

It is not by mere chance that the 'popular' war, with its principles, its strategy, its tactics and its theoreticians, begins at the same time as the industrial powers brought total war to its ultimate stage with the harnessing of nuclear fission. Nor is it by chance that it resulted in the ruin of colonialism. The contradiction that gave victory to the FLN in Algeria was typical of the time; in fact, popular war eradicates classical war (as does the hydrogen bomb).

Against partisans backed by the entire population, colonial armies are helpless. They have only one way of escaping from the harassment which demoralises them and tends towards a Dien Bien Phu. This is to eliminate the civilian population. As it is the unity of a whole people that is containing the conventional army, the only anti-guerrilla strategy which will be effective is the destruction of that people, in other words, the civilians, women and children.

Torture and genocide were the colonialists' answers to the uprising of the natives. And that answer, as we know, is useless if it is not definitive and total. A determined population, unified by its fierce and politicised partisan army, will not let itself be intimidated, as it was in the heyday of colonialism, by a massacre 'as a lesson'. On the contrary, this will only increase its hatred. It is no longer a matter of arousing fear but of physically *liquidating* a people. And as this is not possible without at the same time eliminating the colonial economy and the colonial system; the settlers panic, the colonial powers grow tired of sinking manpower and money into a conflict with no solution, the masses at home end up opposing the continuation of barbaric wars and the colonies become independent states.

There do exist, however, cases where the genocidal solution to popular wars is not held back by innate contradictions. Total genocide then reveals itself as the foundation of anti-guerrilla strategy. And, under certain circumstances, it would even present itself as the ultimate objective, either immediately or gradually. This is exactly what has happened in the war in Vietnam. This is a new aspect of the imperialist process, one usually called neo-colonialism because it is defined as aggression against an old colonial country, which has already attained its independence, to subject it once again to colonial rule. At first, the neo-colonialists make sure – either by the financing of a *putsch* or by another underhand stroke – that the new rulers will not represent the interest of the masses but that of a small minority of the privileged classes and, thus, that of foreign capital. In Vietnam this took the form of Diem, imposed, maintained and armed by the United States, and of the proclaimed decision to reject the Treaty of Geneva and to constitute the Vietnamese territory south of the 17th parallel as an independent state. The natural results of this were a police force and an army to hunt those who, frustrated in their victory, immediately and even *before* any effective resistance movement, declared themselves to be the enemies of the new government. It was the reign of terror that provoked a new uprising in the South and re-ignited the popular war. Did the US ever think that Diem would quash the revolt at its outset? In any event, they did not delay in sending experts, then troops, until they were up to their necks in the conflict. And gradually we can retrace almost exactly the same war that Ho Chi Minh waged against the French, even though the American government declared at the beginning that they were sending their troops out of generosity and out of duty to an ally.

This is how it appears. But, fundamentally, these two successive conflicts do have a different nature: the United States, unlike the French, do not have any economic interests in Vietnam. A few private American companies have invested there, but they are not so large that they could not, if necessary, be sacrificed without really affecting the American economy or harming the monopolies. Because the US is not pursuing the war for *direct* economic reasons, it need not rule out putting an end to it by the ultimate strategy of genocide. This does not prove that America has thought of this solution, only that nothing bars it from such a strategy.

In fact, according to the Americans themselves, the war has two objectives. Recently, Dean Rusk declared: 'We are defending ourselves.' It is no longer Diem, the ally in danger, or Ky that they have come to rescue. It is the *United States* that is in danger in Saigon. This means that their first aim is military: it is to encircle Communist China, the major obstacle to their expansionism. Thus, they will not let south-east Asia escape. America has put men in power in Thailand, it controls part of Laos and threatens to invade Cambodia. But these conquests will be useless if the US has to face a free Vietnam with thirty-one million united people. That is why the military chiefs often talk of 'key positions'. That is why Dean Rusk says, with unconscious humour, that the armed forces of the United States are fighting in Vietnam 'to avoid a Third World War'. Either this phrase makes no sense at all, or it must be understood to mean 'to win a Third World War'. In short, the first objective is governed by the necessity of establishing a *Pacific Defence Line*, which can only be imposed in the general political framework of imperialism.

The second objective is economic. General Westmoreland defined it in these terms in October 1966: 'We are making war in Vietnam to show that guerrilla warfare does not pay.' To show *whom*? The Vietnamese? That would be very surprising. Is it necessary to spend so many human lives and so much money to convince a nation of poor peasants struggling thousands of miles from San Francisco? And, above all, what need was there to *attack*, to provoke to battle and then crush it so as to show the uselessness of the fight, when the interests of the large companies are so negligible? Westmoreland's phrase – like that of Rusk quoted above – needs to be completed. It is to *the others* that they want to prove that guerrilla warfare does not pay: all the exploited and oppressed nations who may be tempted to free themselves from the Yankee yoke with a war for freedom, first of all against their own pseudo-governments and the *compradores* supported by a national army, then against the 'Special Forces' of the United States and finally against the GIs. In other words, it is an example for Latin America and the entire underdeveloped world. To Guevara, who used to say: 'We need many Vietnams', the American government replies: 'They will all be crushed as we are crushing this one.'

In other words, this war is primarily a warning for three, and perhaps four, continents. After all, Greece is also a peasant nation and a dictatorship has just been established there. It is best to warn: submission or complete liquidation. So, this exemplary genocide is a warning to all humanity. It is with this warning that six per cent of mankind hope, without too much expense, to control the remaining ninety-four per cent.

At this point in our discussion, three facts emerge: (1) the US government wants a base and an example; (2) this can be achieved, without any greater obstacle than the resistance of the Vietnamese people themselves, by liquidating an entire people and establishing a Pax Americana on a Vietnamese desert; (3) to attain the second, the US *must* achieve, at least partially, this extermination.

The declarations of American statesmen are not as frank as those that Hitler made in his day. But honesty is not indispensable; the facts speak for themselves. The speeches that accompany them, *ad usum internum*, will only be believed by the American people; the rest of the world understands only too well. Friendly governments keep silent. The others denounce the genocide, but the Americans reply to them that they are showing which side they are really on by their unproven accusations. In fact, say the American government, we have done nothing but offer the Vietnamese – North and South – this choice: either you stop your aggression or we break you. There is no longer any need to point out that this proposition is absurd since the aggression is American, so that only the Americans themselves can put an end to it. But this absurdity is not uncalculated: it is clever to formulate a demand which the Vietnamese cannot possibly satisfy. In this way, America remains the master of the decision to stop the fighting. But, one might read the alternatives as: declare yourselves conquered, or 'we will take you back to the Stone Age'. It does not cancel out the second term of the alternative, which is genocide. They have said: genocide, yes, but only *conditional* genocide. Is this legally valid? Is it even conceivable?

If the argument had any legal meaning, the government of the United States would only just escape the accusation of genocide. But, as Maître Matarasso has remarked, the law, in distinguishing between intention and motive, does not leave room for this escape clause. Genocide, especially as it has been carried on for several years, may well have blackmail as a motive. One may declare that one will stop if the victim submits. Those are the motivations and the act does not cease to be genocide by intention. This is particularly so when, as in this case, part of the group has been annihilated to force the rest to submission.

But let us look more closely and see what the terms of the alternative are. In the South, this is the choice: the villages are burnt, the population has to endure massive and deliberately destructive bombardments, the cattle are shot at, the vegetation is ruined by defoliants, what does grow is ruined by toxic elements, machine guns are aimed haphazardly, and everywhere there is killing, rape and pillage. That is genocide in its most rigorous meaning of massive extermination. What is the other choice? What must the Vietnamese people do to escape this atrocious death? Join the American armed forces or those of Saigon, or let themselves be enclosed in strategic hamlets or in those 'new life' compounds, which are two names for concentration camps.

We know about these camps from numerous witnesses. They are surrounded by barbed wire. The most elementary needs are ignored. There is under-nourishment and complete lack of sanitation. The prisoners are packed into tents or primitive huts where they stifle. The social structure is destroyed. Husbands are separated from wives, mothers from their children, family life – so respected by the Vietnamese – no longer exists. As the homes are broken up, the birth rate diminishes; all possibility of cultural or religious life is abolished. Even work that will improve the standard of living is denied them. These unfortunates are not even slaves (the servile condition of the American Negroes has not stifled their own deep culture); this group is reduced to the state of an appendage, to the worst of vegetative lives. Anyone who wants to escape can only make contact with other men shattered and ravaged by hate, who can only regroup clandestinely for political resistance. The enemy guesses this, so that the camps are raked over two or three times. Even there, security is never certain and the shattering forces are always at work. If by any chance a broken family, e.g. some children with an older sister or a young mother, are freed, they go to swell the proletariat in the towns.

The elder sister or the young mother, without a breadwinner and with so many mouths to feed, sinks to the utmost degradation in prostitution to the enemy. This is the lot of one third of the population in the South, according to Mr Duncanan's evidence. It is the sort of genocide condemned by the Convention of 1948:

Grave damage to physical or mental health of members of the group;
Intentional submission of the group to such conditions of existence as result in total or partial physical damage;
Steps taken to prevent births within the group;
Forcible removal of children ...

In other words, it is not true that the choice lies between death or submission. Submission, under these circumstances, amounts to genocide. Let us say that there is only a choice between immediate violent death and a slow death after mental and physical degradation.

Is it any different in the North?

One choice is *extermination*: not only the daily risk of death but also the systematic destruction of the economic system, from the irrigation ditches to the factories of which 'there must not be a brick left upon another brick'; deliberate attacks on the civilian population, and in particular on the countryside; destruction of hospitals, schools, places of worship, consistent effort towards wiping out the achievements of twenty years of Socialism. Is this simply to terrorise the population? That can only be achieved by the daily extermination of an ever larger number of the group. This terrorism itself, in its psycho-social consequences, is genocide. Who knows if, with the children in particular, this will not result in mental disturbances which will affect them permanently?

The other choice is capitulation. This would mean acceptance from the North Vietnamese that their country should be divided in two and that the American dictatorship, either directly or through their puppets, should be imposed on their compatriots and on the members of their own families from whom the war has separated them. Would this intolerable humiliation put an end to the war? This is far from certain: the NLF [National Liberation Front] and the DRV [Democratic Republic of Vietnam – North Vietnam], although united, have different strategies and tactics because of their different stances in the war. If the NLF continued the struggle, American bombers would carry on, even if the DRV capitulated.

But should the war come to an end, we know – from official declarations – that the United States would be generously inclined to rebuild the DRV with mountains of dollars. This would mean that they would destroy, with their private investments or conditional loans, all the economic basis of socialism. That, too, is genocide: the cutting in two of a sovereign state; occupying one half with a reign of terror, effectively ruining the enterprise so dearly paid for by the other half with economic pressures and with calculated investments, to be held in a tight stranglehold. The national unit of 'Vietnam' would not be physically eliminated, but it would no longer exist economically, politically or culturally.

In the North, as in the South, there is a choice between two types of destruction:

collective death or disintegration. Most significant is the fact that the American government has felt the measure of NLF and DRV resistance: it knows now that only total destruction will be effective. The Front is more powerful than ever; North Vietnam is resolute. For this very reason, the calculated extermination of the Vietnamese people can only be intended to make them capitulate. The Americans offer them peace knowing that it will not be accepted. This spurious alternative hides the real imperialist intention, which is a gradual progress towards the ultimate escalation of total genocide.

The United States government could have achieved this immediately by a Vietnamese *Blitzkrieg*. But, apart from the fact that this extermination would have involved complicated preparations – for example, the construction and unrestricted use of air bases in Thailand, shortening the bombers' journey by 5,000 kilometres – the essential aim of the 'escalation' was and still is, to this day, to prepare bourgeois opinion for genocide. From this point of view, the Americans have succeeded only too well. The repeated and systematic bombing of the densely populated areas of Haiphong and Hanoi, which two years ago would have given rise to violent protests, is carried on today in a sort of general indifference which is more like gangrene than apathy. The trick has worked: public opinion accepts a constant and imperceptible increase of pressure which is preparing their minds for the final genocide. Is this genocide possible? No. But only because of the Vietnamese, their courage and the admirable efficiency of their organisations. As for the US government, nobody can excuse their crime just because the intelligence and heroism of their victims limits its effects.

One can conclude that, in a 'popular' war (that product of our times, the answer to imperialist aggression and the claim to sovereignty of a people conscious of its own unity) only two attitudes are possible: either the aggressor gives way, makes peace and recognises that a whole nation is opposing him; or else, realizing the ineffectiveness of classical strategy, if he can do so without damaging his own interests, he resorts to extermination pure and simple. There is no other choice; but, this choice, at least, is always *possible.*

While the armed forces of the USA are digging deeper into Vietnam, intensifying the massacres and bombings, attempting to subject Laos and intending to invade Cambodia, there is no doubt that the government of the United States, despite all the hypocritical denials, has opted for genocide.

The intention is obvious from the facts. And, as M. Aybar said, it can only be *premeditated.* It is possible that in the past genocide was committed suddenly, in a flash of passion, in the midst of tribal or feudal conflicts. Anti-guerrilla genocide, however, is a product of our times that necessarily entails organisation, bases and, therefore, accomplices (from a distance) and the appropriate budget. It needs to be thought over and planned. Does this mean that those responsible are fully aware of their own intentions? It is difficult to decide: to do so one would have to probe the latent ill-will of puritanical motives.

Maybe some people in the State Department are so used to lying that they still manage to believe that they only want the best for Vietnam. But, after the most recent declarations of their spokesmen, one can presume that there are fewer of these innocents. 'We are defending ourselves: even if the Saigon government asked us to, we would not leave Vietnam', etc. In any case, we do not have to worry about this psychological hide-and-seek. The truth is to be found *on the field*, in the racialism of the American troops. Naturally, this racialism - anti-black, anti-Asiatic, anti-Mexican - is a fundamental characteristic which has deep-rooted origins and which existed, latent or apparent, long before the Vietnam war. The proof lies in the United States government's refusal to ratify the Geneva Convention on genocide. This does not mean that ever since 1948 the Americans have intended to exterminate whole peoples but that, according to their own declaration, the Convention would have conflicted with the internal legislation of many of the American States. In other words, the present leaders consider themselves unshackled in Vietnam today thanks to their predecessors who had wanted to respect the anti-Negro racialism of the South. In any case, ever since 1965, the racialism of the Yankee soldiers from Saigon to the 17th parallel has increased. The young Americans torture without repugnance, shooting at unarmed women for the pleasure of completing a hat-trick: they kick the wounded Vietnamese in the testicles; they cut off the ears of the dead for trophies. The officers are worst: a general was boasting in front of a Frenchman who testified at the Tribunal of hunting the Viet Cong from his helicopter and shooting them down in the rice fields. They were, of course, not NLF fighters, who know how to protect themselves, but peasants working in their rice fields. In these confused American minds the Viet Cong and the Vietnamese tend to become more and more indistinguishable. A common saying is 'The only good Vietnamese is a dead one', or, what comes to the same thing, 'Every dead Vietnamese is a Viet Cong.'

The peasants get ready to harvest the rice south of the 17th parallel. American soldiers come and burn their houses and want to transfer them to a strategic hamlet. The peasants protest. What else can they do bare-handed against these Martians? They say 'The rice is so good; we would like to stay to eat our rice.' No more, but that is enough to exasperate the young Americans: 'It is the Viet Cong who have put this into your heads. It is they who have taught you to resist.' These soldiers are so muddled that they consider as 'subversive' violence the feeble protests that their own violence has provoked. Originally, they were probably disappointed: they came to save Vietnam from Communist aggressors. They soon saw that the Vietnamese actually disliked them. Instead of the attractive role of the liberator they found themselves the occupiers. It was the beginning of self-appraisal: 'They do not want us, we have no business here.' But their protest goes no further: they become angry and simply tell themselves that a Vietnamese is, by definition, a suspect.

There is not a single Vietnamese who is not really a Communist: the proof is their hatred of the Yankees. Here, in the shadowy and robot-like souls of the soldiers, we find the truth about the war in Vietnam: it matches all of Hitler's declarations. He killed the Jews because they were Jews. The armed forces of the United States torture and kill men, women and children in Vietnam *because they are Vietnamese*. Whatever the lies or nervous hedging of the government, the spirit of genocide is in the soldiers' minds. This is their way of enduring the genocidal situation in which their government has put them. The witness Peter Martinsen, a young student of twenty-three who had 'interrogated' prisoners for six months and could not bear his memories, told us: 'I am an average American, I am like any other student, and here I am a war criminal.' And he was right to add: 'Anyone in my place would have acted as I did.'

His only error was to attribute these degrading crimes to the influence of war in general. No: it is not war in the abstract, but war waged by the largest power against a people of poor peasants, and war lived by those who wage it as the only possible relationship between an overdeveloped nation and an underdeveloped one, that is to say genocide expressed through racialism. The only possible relationship, apart from stopping short and leaving.

Total war implies a certain equilibrium of strength, a certain reciprocity. The colonial wars were waged without reciprocity, but colonial interests limited genocide. This present genocide, the latest development of the unequal progress of societies, is total war waged to the end by one side and with not one particle of reciprocity.

The American government is not guilty of having invented modern genocide, nor even of having chosen it from other possible answers to the guerrilla. It is not guilty – for example – of having preferred it on the grounds of strategy or economy. In effect, genocide presents itself as the only possible reaction to the insurrection of a whole people against its oppressors. The American government is guilty of having preferred a policy of war and aggression aimed at total genocide to a policy of peace, the only other alternative, because it would have implied a necessary reconsideration of the principal objectives imposed by the big imperialist companies by means of pressure groups. America is guilty of following through and intensifying the war, although each of its leaders daily understands even better, from the reports of the military chiefs, that the only way to win is to rid Vietnam of all the Vietnamese.

It is guilty of being deceitful, evasive, of lying, and lying to itself, embroiling itself every minute a little more, despite the lessons that this unique and unbearable experience has taught, on a path along which there can be no return. It is guilty, by its own admission, of knowingly conducting this war of 'example' to make genocide a challenge and a threat to all peoples. When a peasant dies in his rice field, cut down by a machine-gun, we are all hit. Therefore, the Vietnamese are fighting for all men and the American forces are fighting all of us. Not just in theory or in the abstract. And not only because genocide is a crime universally condemned by the rights of man. But because, little by little, this genocidal blackmail is spreading to all humanity, adding to the blackmail of atomic war. This crime is perpetrated under our eyes every day, making accomplices out of those who do not denounce it.

In this context, the imperialist genocide can become more serious. For the group that the Americans are trying to destroy by means of the Vietnamese nation is the whole of humanity.

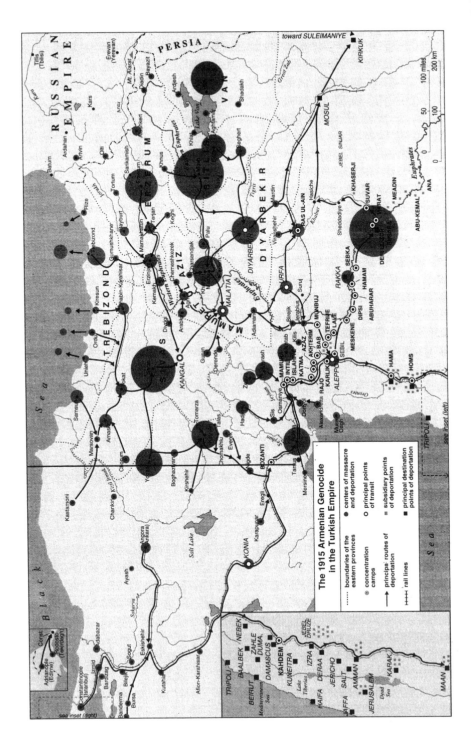

The 1915 Armenian Genocide
in the Turkish Empire

.... boundaries of the
eastern provinces

⊛ concentration
camps

→ principal routes of
deportation

+++ rail lines

● centers of massacre
and deportation

○ principal points
of transit

■ subsidiary points
of deportation

■ principal destination
points of deportation

The First Holocaust

Robert Fisk

This is the first of two instalments from Robert Fisk's most compelling book, The Great War for Civilisation: The Conquest of the Middle East *(Harper Perennial £9.99). It is reprinted here with grateful acknowledgements to the author for his kind permission to do so. A second part will appear in* Spokesman 94.

Pile the bodies high at Austerlitz and Waterloo
Shovel them under and let me work –
    I am the grass; I cover all.
And pile them high at Gettysburg
And pile them high at Ypres and Verdun.
Shovel them under and let me work.
Two years, ten years, and passengers ask the
    conductor:
    What place is this?
    Where are we now?

I am the grass,
Let me work.

CARL SANDBURG, 'Grass'

The hill of Margada is steep and littered with volcanic stones, a place of piercing bright light and shadows high above the eastern Syrian desert. It is cold on the summit and the winter rains have cut fissures into the mud between the rocks, brown canyons of earth that creep down to the base of the hill. Far below, the waters of the Habur slink between grey, treeless banks, twisting through dark sand dunes, a river of black secrets. You do not need to know what happened at Margada to find something evil in this place. Like the forests of eastern Poland, the Hill of Margada is a place of eradicated memory, although the local Syrian police constable, a man of bright cheeks and generous moustache, had heard that something terrible happened here long before he was born.

It was the *Independent's* photographer, Isabel Ellsen, who found the dreadful evidence. Climbing down the crack cut into the hill by the rain, she brushed her hand against the brown earth and found herself looking at a skull, its cranium dark brown, its teeth still shiny. To its left a backbone protruded through the mud. When I scraped away the earth on the other side of the crevasse, an entire skeleton was revealed, and then another, and a third, so closely packed that the bones had become tangled among each other. Every few inches of mud would reveal a femur, a skull, a set of teeth, fibula and sockets, squeezed together, as tightly packed as they had been on the day they died in terror in 1915, roped together to drown in their thousands.

Exposed to the air, the bones became soft and claylike and flaked away in our hands, the last mortal remains of an entire race of people disappearing as swiftly as their Turkish oppressors would have wished us to forget them. As many as 50,000 Armenians were murdered in this little killing field, and it took a minute or two before Ellsen and I fully comprehended that we were standing in a mass grave. For Margada and the Syrian desert around it – like thousands of villages in what was Turkish Armenia – are the Auschwitz of the Armenian people, the place of the world's first, forgotten, Holocaust.

The parallel with Auschwitz is no idle one. Turkey's reign of terror against the Armenian people was an attempt to destroy the Armenian race. The Armenian death toll was almost a million and a half. While the Turks spoke publicly of the need to 'resettle' their Armenian population – as the Germans were to speak later of the Jews of Europe – the true intentions of the Turkish government were quite specific. On 15 September 1915, for example – and a carbon of this document exists – the Turkish interior minister, Talaat Pasha, cabled an instruction to his prefect in Aleppo. 'You have already been informed that the Government ... has decided to destroy completely all the indicated persons living in Turkey ... Their existence must be terminated, however tragic the measures taken may be, and no regard must be paid to either age or sex, or to any scruples of conscience.'

Was this not exactly what Himmler told his SS murderers in 1941? Here on the hill of Margada we were now standing among what was left of the 'indicated persons'. And Boghos Dakessian, who along with his five-year-old nephew Hagop had driven up to the Habur with us from the Syrian town of Deir es-Zour, knew all about those 'tragic measures'. 'The Turks brought whole families up here to kill them. It went on for days. They would tie them together in lines, men, children, women, most of them starving and sick, many naked. Then they would push them off the hill into the river and shoot one of them. The dead body would then carry the others down and drown them. It was cheap that way. It cost only one bullet.'

Dakessian knelt beside the small ravine and, with a car key, gently prised the earth from another skull. If this seems morbid, even obscene, it must be remembered that the Armenian people have lived with this for nine decades – and that the evidence of evil outweighs sensitivity. When he had scraped the earth from the eye sockets and the teeth, Dakessian handed the skull to little Hagop, who stood in the ditch, smiling, unaware of the meaning of death. 'I have told him what happened here,' Dakessian says. 'He must learn to understand.' Hagop was named after his great-grandfather – Boghos Dakessian's grandfather – who was himself a victim of the first Holocaust of the twentieth century, beheaded by a Turkish gendarme in the town of Marash in 1915.

In Beirut back in 1992, in the Armenian home for the blind – where the last survivors had lived with their memories through the agony of Lebanon's sixteen-year civil war, I would discover Zakar Berberian, in a room devoid of light, a single electric bar vainly struggling with the frosty interior. The 89-year-old Armenian cowered in an old coat, staring intently at his visitors with sightless eyes. Within ten years Zakar Berberian – like almost all those who gave me their testimony of genocide – was dead. But here is his story, just as he told it to me:

> I was twelve years old in 1915 and lived in Balajik on the Euphrates. I had four brothers. My father was a barber. What I saw on the day the Turkish gendarmes came to our village I will never forget. I had not yet lost my eyesight. There was a market place in Balajik which had been burned down and there were stones and building bricks on the ground. I saw with my own eyes what happened. The men were ordered to leave the village – they were taken away and never seen again. The women and children were told to go to the old market. The soldiers came then and in front of the mothers, they picked up each child – maybe the child was six or seven or eight – and they threw them up in the air and let them drop on the old stones. If they survived, the Turkish soldiers picked them up again by their feet and beat their brains out on the stones. They did all this, you see? In front of their mothers. I have never heard such screaming ... From our barber's shop, I saw all these scenes. The Turkish soldiers were in uniform and they had the gendarmerie of the government with them. Of course, the mothers could do nothing when their children were killed like this. They just shouted and cried. One of the children was in our school. They found his school book in his pocket which showed he had the highest marks in class. They beat his brains out. The Turks tied one of my friends by his feet to the tail of a horse and dragged him out of the village until he died.
>
> There was a Turkish officer who used to come to our shop. He sheltered my brother who had deserted from the army but he said we must all flee, so we left Balajik for the town of Asma. We survived then because my father changed his religion. He agreed to become a Muslim. But both my father and my mother got sick. I think it was cholera. They died and I was also sick and like a dead person. The deportations went on and I should have died but a Turk gave me food to survive.

Berberian was eventually taken to a children's orphanage.

> They gave me a bath but the water was dirty. There had been children in the same bath who had glaucoma. So I bathed in the water and I too went blind. I have seen nothing since. I have waited ever since for my sight to be given back to me. But I know why I went blind. It was not the bath. It was because my father changed his religion. God took his revenge on me because we forsook him.

Perhaps it was because of his age that Berberian betrayed no emotion in his voice. He would never see again. His eyes were missing, a pale green skin covering what should have been his pupils.

So terrible was the year 1915 in the Armenian lands of Turkey and in the deserts of northern Syria and so cruel were the Turkish authorities of the time that it is necessary to remember that Muslims sometimes risked their lives for the doomed Armenian Christians. In almost every interview I concluded with the elderly, blind Armenians who survived their people's genocide, there were stories of individual Turks who, driven by religion or common humanity, disobeyed the quasi-fascist laws of the Young Turk rulers in Constantinople and sheltered

Armenians in their homes, treating Armenian Christian orphans as members of their own Muslim families. The Turkish governor of Deir es-Zour, Ali Suad Bey, was so kind to the Armenian refugees – he set up orphanages for the children – that he was recalled to Constantinople and replaced by Zeki Bey, who turned the town into a concentration camp.

The story of the Armenian genocide is one of almost unrelieved horror at the hands of Turkish soldiers and policemen who enthusiastically carried out their government's orders to exterminate a race of Christian people in the Middle East. In 1915, Ottoman Turkey was at war with the Allies and claimed that its Armenian population – already subjected to persecution in the 1894-6 massacres – was supporting Turkey's Christian enemies. At least 200,000 Armenians from Russian Armenia were indeed fighting in the Tsarist army. In Beirut, Levon Isahakian – blind but alert at an incredible 105 years old – still bore the scar of a German cavalry sabre on his head, received when he was a Tsarist infantryman in Poland in 1915. In the chaos of the Bolshevik revolution two years later, he made his way home; he trudged across Russia on foot to Nagorno-Karabakh, sought refuge in Iran, was imprisoned by the British in Baghdad and finally walked all the way to Aleppo, where he found the starving remnants of his own Armenian people. He had been spared. But thousands of Armenians had also been serving in the Ottoman forces; they would not be so lucky. The Turks alleged that Armenians had given assistance to Allied naval fleets in the Mediterranean, although no proof of this was ever produced.

The reality was that a Young Turk movement – officially the 'Committee of Union and Progress' – had effectively taken control of the corrupt Ottoman empire from Sultan Abdul Hamid. Originally a liberal party to which many Armenians gave their support, it acquired a nationalistic, racist, pan-Turkic creed which espoused a Turkish-speaking Muslim nation stretching from Ankara to Baku – a dream that was briefly achieved in 1918 but which is today physically prevented only by the existence of the post-Soviet Armenian republic. The Christian Armenians of Asia Minor, a mixture of Persian, Roman and Byzantine blood, swiftly became disillusioned with the new rulers of the Turkish empire.[1]

Encouraged by their victory over the Allies at the Dardanelles, the Turks fell upon the Armenians with the same fury as the Nazis were to turn upon the Jews of Europe two decades later. Aware of his own disastrous role in the Allied campaign against Turkey, Winston Churchill was to write in *The Aftermath* – a volume almost as forgotten today as the Armenians themselves – that 'it may well be that the British attack on the Gallipoli Peninsula stimulated the merciless fury of the Turkish government.' Certainly, the Turkish victory at the Dardanelles over the British and Australian armies – Private Charles Dickens, who peeled Maude's proclamation from the wall in Baghdad, was there, and so was Frank Wills, the man my father refused to execute in 1919 – gave a new and ruthless self-confidence to the Turkish regime. It chose 24 April 1915 – for ever afterwards commemorated as the day of Armenian genocide – to arrest and murder all the leading Armenian intellectuals of Constantinople. They followed this pogrom with the wholesale and systematic destruction of the Armenian race in Turkey.

Armenian soldiers in the Ottoman army had already been disbanded and converted into labour battalions by the spring of 1915. In the Armenian home for the blind in Beirut, 91-year-old Nevart Srourian held out a photograph of her father, a magnificent, handsome man in a Turkish army uniform. Nevart was almost deaf when I met her in 1992. 'My father was a wonderful man, very intelligent,' she shouted at me in a high-pitched voice. 'When the Turks came for our family in 1915, he put his old uniform back on and my mother sewed on badges to pretend he had high rank. He wore the four medals he had won as a soldier. Dressed like this, he took us all to the railway station at Konya and put us on a train and we were saved. But he stayed behind. The Turks discovered what he had done. They executed him.'

In every town and village, all Armenian men were led away by the police, executed by firing squad and thrown into mass graves or rivers. Mayreni Kaloustian was eighty-eight when I met her, a frail creature with her head tied in a cloth, who physically shook as she told her story in the Beirut blind home, an account of such pathos that one of the young Armenian nursing staff broke down in tears as she listened to it.

I come from Mush. When the snow melted each year, we planted rye. My father, Manouk Tarouian, and my brother worked in the fields. Then the Turkish soldiers came. It was 1915. They put all the men from the village, about a thousand, in a stable and next morning they took them from Mush – all my male relatives, my cousins and brothers. My father was among them. The Turks said: 'The government needs you.' They took them like cattle. We don't know where they took them. We saw them go. Everybody was in a kind of shock. My mother Khatoun found out what happened. There was a place near Mush where three rivers come together and pass under one bridge. It is a huge place of water and sand. My mother went there in the morning and saw hundreds of our men lined up on the bridge, face to face. Then the soldiers shot at them from both sides. She said the Armenians 'fell on top of each other like straw'. The Turks took the clothes and valuables off the bodies and then they took the bodies by the hands and feet and threw them into the water. All day they lined up the men from Mush like this and it went on until nightfall. When my mother returned to us, she said: 'We should return to the river and throw ourselves in.'

What Mayreni was describing was no isolated war crime. It was a routine. At the Kemakh Gorge, Kurds and troops of the Turkish 86th Cavalry Brigade butchered more than 20,000 women and children. At Bitlis, the Turks drowned more than 900 women in the Tigris river. So great was the slaughter near the town of Erzinjan that the thousands of corpses in the Euphrates formed a barrage that forced the river to change course for a hundred metres.

The American ambassador to Constantinople, Henry Morgenthau, himself a Jew, described what happened next in a telegram to the US State Department:

Reports from widely scattered districts indicate systematic attempt to uproot peaceful Armenian populations and through arbitrary arrests, terrible tortures, wholesale expulsions and deportations from one end of the Empire to the other accompanied by frequent instances of rape, pillage, and murder, turning into massacre, to bring destruction and destitution on them. These measures are not in response to popular or fanatical demand but are purely arbitrary and directed from Constantinople in the name of military necessity, often in districts where no military operations are likely to take place.

Mayreni Kaloustian, along with her mother Khatoun, her sisters Megad, Dilabar, Heriko and Arzoun and her two youngest brothers Drjivan and Feryad, set off on the death march from Mush the day after the men were murdered at the river.

> First we travelled in carts hauled by bulls. Then we had to walk for so many weeks. There were thousands of us. We begged food and water. It was hot. We walked from the spring and we did not stop until St Jacob's Day, in December. I was only twelve and one day I lost my mother. I did not see her again. We went to Sivas. Then the Russians came, the army of the Tsar, and they reached Mush and blew up the bridge where my father was killed. We tried to go back to Mush but the Russians were defeated. Then my brothers and sisters and I all caught cholera. They died except for Arzoun and myself. I lost her, too. I was taken to an orphanage. You can never know what our life was like. The Turks let the bandits do what they wanted. The Kurds were allowed to kidnap the beautiful girls. I remember they took them away on horses, slung over the saddles. They took children. The Turks made us pay for water.

It is now largely forgotten that the Turks encouraged one of their Muslim ethnic groups to join them in this slaughter. Thus tens of thousands of Armenians were massacred – amid scenes of rape and mass pillage – by the Kurds, the very people upon whom Saddam Hussein would attempt genocide just over sixty years later. On the banks of the Habur river not far from Margada, Armenian women were sold to Kurds and Arab Muslims. Survivors related that the men paid 20 piastres for virgins but only 5 piastres for children or women who had already been raped. The older women, many of them carrying babies, were driven into the river to drown.

In 1992, 160 kilometres south of Margada, in a hamlet of clay huts 30 kilometres from the Iraqi frontier – so close that in 1991 the Syrian villagers could watch Saddam's Scud missiles trailing fire as they were launched into the night skies above their homes – I found old Serpouhi Papazian, survivor of the Armenian genocide, widow of an Arab Muslim who rescued her at Deir es-Zour. A stick-like woman of enormous energy, with bright eyes and no teeth, she thought she was a hundred years old – she was in fact ninety-two – but there could be no doubting her story.

> I come from Takirda, twelve hours by horse from Istanbul. I was fifteen at the time. The Turks drove us from our home and all my family were put on a filthy ship that brought us from Konya to the coast and then we went to Aleppo – my mother Renouhi and my father Tatios, my aunt Azzaz and my sisters Hartoui and Yeva. They beat us and starved us. At Aleppo, my mother and Auntie Azzaz died of sickness. They made us walk all the way to Deir es-Zour in the summer heat. We were kept in a camp there by the Turks. Every day, the Turks came and took thousands of Armenians from there to the north. My father heard terrible stories of families being murdered together so he tattooed our initials in the Armenian alphabet on our wrists so that we could find each other later.

Tattooed identities. The grim parallels with another genocide did not occur to old Serpouhi Papazian. She was rescued by an Arab boy and, like so many of the Armenian women who sought refuge with non-Turkish Muslims, she converted to Islam. Only later did she hear what happened to the rest of her family.

> The Turks sent them all north into the desert. They tied them together with many other people. My father and my sisters were tied together, Yeva and Hartoui by their wrists. Then they took them to a hill at a place called Margada where there were many bodies. They threw them into the mud of the river and shot one of them – I don't know which – and so they all drowned there together.

Ten years after the Armenian Holocaust, Serpouhi returned to the hill at Margada to try to find the remains of her father and sisters. 'All I found in 1925 were heaps of bones and skulls,' she said. 'They had been eaten by wild animals and dogs. I don't even know why you bother to come here with your notebook and take down what I say.' And Boghos Dakessian, in a bleak moment among the place of skulls on Margada hill, said much the same thing. One of the skulls he was holding collapsed into dust in his hands. 'Don't say "pity them",' he told us. 'It is over for them. It is finished.' Serpouhi remembered the river running beside the hill – but Isabel Ellsen and I had at first found no trace of bones along the banks of the Habur river. It was only when we climbed the hill above the main road to Deir es-Zour – almost 2 kilometres from the water – to survey the landscape, that we made out, faintly below us, the banks of a long-dried-up river. The Habur had changed its course over the previous seventy-five years and had moved more than a kilometre eastward. That is when Isobel found the skulls. We were standing on the hill where Yeva and Hartoui were murdered with their father. And it occurred to me that, just as the Euphrates had changed course after its waters became clogged with bodies, so here too the Habur's waters might have become choked with human remains and moved to the east. Somewhere in the soft clay of Margada, the bodies of Yeva and Hartoui lie to this day.

But the Armenian killing fields are spread wide over the Syrian desert. Eighty kilometres to the north, east of the village of Shedadi, lies another little Auschwitz, a cave into which Turkish troops drove thousands of Armenian men during the deportations. Boghos Dakessian and I found it quite easily in the middle of what is now a Syrian oilfield. Part of the cave has long since collapsed, but it was still possible to crawl into the mouth of the rock and worm our way with the aid of a cigarette lighter into its ominous interior. It stretched for over a kilometre underground. 'They killed about five thousand of our people here,' Dakessian said with a statistician's annoyance at such imprecision. 'They stuffed them in the cave and then started a bonfire here at the mouth and filled the cave with smoke. They were asphyxiated. They all coughed till they died.'

It took several seconds before the historical meaning of all this became apparent. Up here, in the cold, dry desert, the Turks turned this crack in the earth's crust into the twentieth century's first gas chamber. The principles of technological genocide began here in the Syrian desert, at the tiny mouth of this innocent cave, in a natural chamber in the rock.

There are other parallels. Enver Pasha, the Turkish war minister,[2] told Morgenthau that the Armenians were being sent to 'new quarters', just as the Nazis later claimed that the Jews of Europe were being sent east for 'resettlement'. Armenian churches were burned like the synagogues of Nazi Europe. The Armenians died on what the Turks called 'caravans' or 'convoys', just as the Jews of Europe were sent on 'transports' to the death camps. In southern Turkey, the Turks did sometimes use railway cattle wagons to herd Armenian men to their mass graves. The Kurds played the same role of executioners for the Turks that Lithuanians and Ukrainians and Croatians would later assume for the Nazis. The Turks even formed a 'Special Organisation' – *Teshkilat-i Makhsusiye* – to carry out exterminations, an Ottoman predecessor to Hitler's *Einsatzgruppen*, the German 'Special Action Groups'.

Armenian scholars have compiled a map of their people's persecution every bit as detailed as the maps of Europe that show the railway routes to Auschwitz-Birkenau, Treblinka, Dachau and the other Nazi camps. The Armenians in Sivas were driven to Malatya, from Malatya to Aleppo; or from Mush to Diyarbakir to Ras ul-Ain or – via Mardin – to Mosul and Kirkuk. It is a flow chart of suffering, some of the 'convoys' of humiliation and grief driven 150 kilometres south from Marash to Aleppo, then another 300 kilometres east to Deir es-Zour and then north – back in the direction of Turkey for another 150 kilometres up the Habur river and past the hill of Margada. Armenians were deported from the Black Sea coast and from European Turkey to the Syrian desert, some of them moved all the way south to Palestine.

What was at once apparent about this ethnic atrocity was not just its scale – perhaps two hundred thousand Armenians had been slaughtered two decades earlier – but the systematic nature of the Holocaust. A policy of race murder had been devised in wartime by senior statesmen who controlled, as one historian phrased it, the 'machinery of violence, both formal and informal'. Like the Jews of Europe, many Armenians were highly educated; they were lawyers, civil servants, businessmen, journalists. Unlike the Jewish Holocaust, however, the world knew of the Turkish genocide almost as soon as it began. Viscount James Bryce and the young Arnold Toynbee were commissioned to prepare a report for the British government in 1915, and their work, *The Treatment of Armenians in the Ottoman Empire 1915-1916* – 700 pages of eyewitness accounts of the massacres – was to become not only a formative history of the slaughter but the first serious attempt to deal with crimes against humanity. Much of the testimony came from American missionaries in Turkey – the 'non-governmental organisations' of the era – and from Italian, Danish, Swedish, Greek, US and German diplomats and records.[3]

US diplomats were among the first to record the Armenian Holocaust – and among the bravest eyewitnesses – and their accounts in State Department archives remain among the most unimpeachable testimonies of the Armenians' fate. Leslie Davis, the 38-year-old former lawyer who was American consul in Harput, has left us a terrifying account of his own horseback journeys through the dead lands of Armenia. Around Lake Goeljuk and in the space of just twenty-four hours, he saw 'the remains of not less than ten thousand Armenians'. He found corpses piled on rocks at the foot of cliffs, corpses in the water and in the sand, corpses filling up huge ravines; 'nearly all the women lay flat on their backs and showed signs of barbarous mutilation by bayonets of the gendarmes ...' On one of his excursions, Davis came across a dying Armenian woman. When she was offered bread, she 'cried out that she wanted to die'. An Armenian college teacher called Donabed Lulejian who was rescued by Davis passed through a village littered with the bodies of men, women and children, and wrote an essay of pain and dignity – a 'benediction', in the words of the Armenian historian Peter Balakian:

> At least a handful of earth for these slain bodies, for these whitened bones! A handful of earth, at least, for these unclaimed dead ...
> We dislike to fancy the bodies of our dear ones worm-ridden; their eyes, their lovely eyes, filled with worms; their cheeks, their kiss-deserving cheeks, mildewed; their pomegranate-like lips food for reptiles.
> But here they are in the mountains, unburied and forlorn, attacked by worms and scorpions, the eyes bare, the faces horrible amid a loathsome stench, like the odour of the slaughter-house ...
> There are women with breasts uncovered and limbs bare. A handful of earth to shield their honour! ... Give, God, the handful of earth requested of Thee.

Germans, too, bore witness to the massacres because officers of the Kaiser's army had been seconded to Turkey to help reorganise the Ottoman military. Armin Wegner, a German nurse and a second lieutenant in the retinue of Field Marshal von der Goltz, disobeyed orders by taking hundreds of photographs of Armenian victims in the camps at Ras al-Ain, Rakka, Aleppo and Deir es-Zour. Today these fearful pictures of the dead and dying comprise the core of witness images. The Germans were also involved in building Turkey's railway system and saw with their own eyes the first use of cattle trucks for human deportation, men packed ninety to a wagon – the same average the Germans achieved in their transports to the Nazi death camps – on the Anatolian and Baghdad railways. Franz Gunther, a Deutsche Bank representative in Constantinople – the bank was financing the Turkish railway projects – sent a photograph of a deportation train to one of his directors as an example of the Ottoman government's 'bestial cruelty'.

Across the world – and especially in the United States – newspapers gave immense prominence to the genocide. From the start, the *New York Times* distinguished itself with near daily coverage of the slaughter, rape, dispossession and extermination of the Armenians. Its first reports appeared in the paper in November 1914. 'Erzerum fanatics slay Christians,' ran a headline on 29 November. Ambassador Morgenthau's representations to the Turkish government were published on 28 April 1915, under the words 'Appeal to Turkey to stop massacres'. By 4 October, the *New York Times* was headlining 'Horrors done in Armenia' above a long dispatch containing details of atrocities, of torture, deportations and child-killing. On 7 October the paper's headline ran '800,000 Armenians counted destroyed ... 10,000 drowned at once'. Morgenthau's memoranda and Bryce's speeches to the House of Lords were given huge coverage. *The Nation* carried a series of powerful editorials, calling upon Berlin

– the United States still being a neutral in the war – to stop the killings by its Turkish ally. Narratives of the mass murders were still being published in the *New York Times* in June 1919, almost eight months after the war ended; 'Armenian girls tell of massacres', read the paper's headline on 1 June. Even in the Canadian city of Halifax, the local paper carried almost weekly reports on the genocide. A volume containing dispatches on the destruction of the Armenians which appeared in the *Halifax Herald* runs to 352 pages.

Rarely have ethnic cleansing and genocidal killings been given publicity on this scale. British diplomats across the Middle East were themselves receiving first-hand accounts of the massacres. In the former Ottoman city of Basra, Gertrude Bell, who would later be Britain's 'Oriental Secretary' in Baghdad, was filing an intelligence report on the outrages received from a captured Turkish soldier.

> The battalion left Aleppo on 3 February and reached Ras al-Ain in twelve hours ... some 12,000 Armenians were concentrated under the guardianship of some hundreds of Kurds ... These Kurds were called gendarmes, but in reality mere butchers; bands of them were publicly ordered to take parties of Armenians, of both sexes, to various destinations, but had secret instructions to destroy the males, children and old women ... One of these gendarmes confessed to killing 100 Armenian men himself ... the empty desert cisterns and caves were also filled with corpses ... The Turkish officers of the battalion were horrified by the sights they saw, and the regimental chaplain (a Muslim divine) on coming across a number of bodies prayed that the divine punishment of these crimes should be averted from Muslims, and by way of expiation, himself worked at digging three graves ... No man can ever think of a woman's body except as a matter of horror, instead of attraction, after Ras al-Ain.

Even after the United States entered the war, its diplomats continued to compile reports on the atrocities. J. B. Jackson, formerly the American consul in Aleppo, wrote in July 1915 of a group of more than 1,000 women and children from Harput who were handed over to Kurds:

> who rode among them, selecting the best-looking women, girls and children ... Before carrying off those finally selected and subdued, they stripped most of the remaining women of their clothes, thereby forcing them to continue the rest of their journey in a nude condition. I was told by eyewitnesses to this outrage that over 300 women arrived at Ras al-Ain ... entirely naked, their hair flowing in the air like wild beasts, and after traveling six days afoot in the burning sun ... some of them personally came to the Consulate [in Aleppo] and exhibited their bodies to me, burned to the color of a green olive, the skin peeling off in great blotches, and many of them carrying gashes on the head and wounds on the body ...

The Armenian Holocaust was recorded, too, in countless private letters and diaries – some of them still unpublished – written by Europeans who found themselves in Ottoman northern Syria and southern Turkey. Here, for example, is an extract from a long account written by Cyril Barter, a British businessman who was sent out of Iraq to Aleppo under Turkish guard in 1915:

I may tell you that two days south of Deir [es-Zour] we met the first fringe of Armenian refugees, and for the next three months I was seeing them continually. To attempt to describe their plight would be impossible. In a few words, there were no men of between sixteen and sixty among them, they had all been massacred on leaving their homes, and these, the remainder, old men, women and children were dying like flies from starvation and disease, having been on the road from their villages to this, the bare desert, with no means of subsistence, for anything from three to six months … It was a nightmare to me for a long time afterwards.

Barter would later submit a report to the Bryce Commission – which originally printed it anonymously – in which he recorded how carts would be taken through Aleppo for newly dead Armenians, the bodies 'thrown into them as one would throw a sack of coal'. Barter, too, would be a witness to the railway deportations, describing how Turks would drive Armenians from their places of refuge and 'hustle them down to the railway station, pack them into the trucks like cattle and forward them to Damascus and different towns in the Hidjaz'.

A British prisoner of war in Turkey, Lieutenant E. H. Jones, was to recall the fate of the Armenians of Yozgat, where he himself was held in a POW camp. 'The butchery had taken place in a valley some dozen miles outside the town,' he wrote. 'Amongst our sentries were men who had slain men, women, and children till their arms were too tired to strike. They boasted of it amongst themselves. And yet, in many ways, they were pleasant enough fellows.' As late as 1923, an Irish schoolboy, John de Courcy Ireland, the future nautical writer and historian, would visit Castel Gandolfo outside Rome, where he would see Armenian refugee children, 'dark, fascinating to look at but very quiet in spite of the disorder in which they swarmed'.

As the survivors of the Armenian Holocaust have died, so their children have taken up their story. A number of Armenians not only escaped death in the 1915 deportations but were confronted by a second massacre in the Greek-held Turkish city of Smyrna – now Izmir – in 1922. 'My father, Sarkis, not only survived the Syrian desert but barely made it out of Smyrna alive,' his daughter Ellen Sarkisian Chesnut wrote to me.

> … he and two friends came to Smyrna just when Attaturk [*sic*] and his men had taken it over. Arrested and taken to a massacre railway yard with several hundred Greeks and Armenians, they were subjected to rounds and rounds of machine gun fire. He survived the onslaught because he fainted. Later he was not so lucky when with fixed bayonets the Turkish soldiers repeatedly stabbed the dead and dying. Wounded badly on his forehead and leg, he nevertheless got up and made for the quay.
>
> Ahead of him he saw two young girls trembling with fright and dazed by what they had seen. He could not leave them there. He grabbed ahold of their hands and the three of them ran for their lives. What they saw on the quay would stay with my father for the rest of his days. Tens of thousands of people crammed together in terror, with the flames of the dying city drawing ever closer. And yet … there was no help forthcoming from the British, French and American warships. But, in the distance, my dad saw that another ship was taking people on board. The three of them would have to jump into the water and swim for it. They did and were rescued by Italian sailors.

The first writer to call the Armenian genocide a holocaust was Winston Churchill, including in a list of Turkish wartime atrocities the 'massacring [of] uncounted thousands of helpless Armenians, men, women and children together, whole districts blotted out in one administrative holocaust ... beyond human redress'. For Churchill:

> the clearance of the race from Asia Minor was about as complete as such an act could be ... There is no reasonable doubt that this crime was planned and executed for political reasons. The opportunity presented itself for clearing Turkish soil of a Christian race opposed to all Turkish ambitions, cherishing national ambitions that could be satisfied only at the expense of Turkey, and planted geographically between Turkish and Caucasian Moslems.

Acknowledging that British and American interest in the 'infamous' massacre of the Armenians 'was lighted by the lamps of religion, philanthropy and politics', Churchill said that the atrocities 'stirred the ire of simple and chivalrous men and women spread widely about the English-speaking world'.

But there were other, less chivalrous men whose interest in the Armenian Holocaust – gleaned at first hand – would prove to be a useful experience in a new and brutal Europe. Franz von Papen, for example, was chief of staff of the Fourth Turkish Army during the 1914-18 war and served as Hitler's vice chancellor in 1933. During the Second World War, he was the Third Reich's ambassador to Turkey. Another German who knew the intimate details of the Armenian genocide was Lieutenant General Hans von Seeckt, who was chief of the Ottoman General Staff in 1917. He laid the groundwork for the *Wehrmacht* in the 1920s and was honoured by Hitler with a state funeral on his death in 1936. Much more sinister was the identity of a young German called Rudolf Hoess, who joined the German forces in Turkey as a teenager. In 1940 he was appointed commandant of Auschwitz, and he became deputy inspector of all Nazi concentration camps at SS headquarters in 1944.

In a work of remarkable scholarship, the Armenian historian Vahakn Dadrian identified Max Erwin von Scheubner-Richter as one of the most effective Nazi mentors. Scheubner-Richter was German vice-consul in Erzerum and witnessed Turkish massacres of Armenians in Bitlis province, writing a long report on the killings for the German chancellor. In all, he submitted to Berlin fifteen reports on the deportations and mass killings, stating in his last message that with the exception of a few hundred thousand survivors, the Armenians of Turkey had been exterminated (*ausgerottet*). He described the methods by which the Turks concealed their plans for the genocide, the techniques used to entrap Armenians, the use of criminal gangs, and even made a reference to the Armenians as 'these "Jews of the Orient" who are wily businessmen'. Scheubner-Richter met Hitler only five years later and would become one of his closest advisers, running a series of racist editorials in a Munich newspaper which called for a 'ruthless and relentless' campaign against Jews so that Germany should be 'cleansed'. When Hitler staged his attempted coup against the Bavarian government, Scheubner-Richter linked arms with Hitler as they marched through the streets and was shot in the heart and killed instantly by a police bullet.

We do not know how much Hitler learned of the Armenian Holocaust from his friend, but he was certainly aware of its details, referring to the genocide first in 1924 when he said that Armenians were the victims of cowardice. Then in August 1939 he asked his rhetorical and infamous question of his generals – in relation to Poles – 'Who after all is today speaking of the destruction of the Armenians?' There have been repeated attempts – especially by Turkey – to pretend that Hitler never made such a remark but Dadrian has found five separate versions of the question, four of them identical; two were filed in German High Command archives. Furthermore, German historians have discovered that Hitler made an almost identical comment in a 1931 interview with a German newspaper editor, saying that 'everywhere people are awaiting a new world order. We intend to introduce a great resettlement policy … remember the extermination of the Armenians.' And there came another fateful reference to the century's first genocide when Hitler was demanding that the Jews of Hungary be deported; he ended a tirade to Admiral Horthy, the Hungarian regent, in 1943 with a remark about 'the downfall of a people who were once so proud – the Persians, who now lead a pitiful existence as Armenians'.

Historical research into the identity of Germans who witnessed the destruction of the Armenians and their later role in Hitler's war is continuing. Some Armenian slave labourers – male and female – spent their last months working to complete a section of the German-run Baghdad railway and were briefly protected by their German supervisors. But other German nationals watched the Armenians die – and did nothing.[4] What was so chilling about Hitler's question to his generals, however, was not just his comparison – the whole world knew the details of the Turkish destruction of its Armenian population – but his equally important knowledge that the perpetrators of these war crimes were rewarded with impunity.

In the immediate aftermath of the First World War, Turkish courts martial were held to punish those responsible and Turkish parliamentarians confessed to crimes against humanity. A Turkish military tribunal, unprecedented in Ottoman history, produced government records that were used as evidence at the trial. One exchange over the telegraph had a Nazi ring to it. An official says of the Armenians: 'They were dispatched to their ultimate destination.' A second voice asks: 'Meaning what?' And the reply comes back: 'Meaning massacred. Killed.' Three minor officials were hanged. The triumvirate itself – Jemal, Enver and Talaat – was sentenced to death *in absentia*.

But the Turkish courts lacked the political will to continue, and the Western allies, who had boldly promised a trial of the major Turkish war criminals – the Armenian mass killings were described as 'crimes against humanity' in an Allied warning to the Ottoman government in May 1915 – lacked the interest to compel them to do so. Indeed, what was to come – the systematic attempt, which continues to this day, to deny that the mass killings were ever perpetrated – is almost as frightening as the powerlessness of the Allies who should have prosecuted those who devised the Armenian genocide. Talaat Pasha, the former interior minister, was assassinated in Berlin by an Armenian whose family had died in the genocide. Soghomon

Tehlirian's trial and subsequent acquittal in 1921 meant that details of the Armenian Holocaust were widely known to the German public. Franz Werfel, the German-Jewish novelist, wrote a prophetic warning of the next Holocaust in his account of Armenian resistance to the Turkish killers, *Forty Days of Musa Dagh*. He lectured across Germany in 1933, only to be denounced by the Nazi newspaper *Das Schwarze Korps* as a propagandist of 'alleged Turkish horrors perpetrated against the Armenians'. The same paper – and here was another disturbing link between the Armenian Holocaust and the Jewish Holocaust still to come – condemned 'America's Armenian Jews for promoting in the USA the sale of Werfel's book'.

Already, the century's first genocide was being 'disappeared'. Winston Churchill continued to emphasise its reality. In 1933, the same year that Werfel toured Germany, Churchill wrote that:

> the Armenian people emerged from the Great War scattered, extirpated in many districts, and reduced through massacre, losses of war and enforced deportations adopted as an easy system of killing ... the Armenians and their tribulations were well known throughout England and the United States ... Their persecutors and tyrants had been laid low by war or revolution. The greatest nations in the hour of their victory were their friends, and would see them righted.

But the Armenians would be betrayed. The archives tell a bitter story of weakness and impotence and false promises. Here, for example, is Clause 1d of the Treaty of Sèvres between the Allied and Ottoman governments of 10 August 1920:

> Turkey recognised Armenia as an independent state, and consented to accept President [Woodrow] Wilson's arbitration with regard to the boundary between the two states.

And here is Article 64 of the same treaty:

> If within one year ... the Kurdish peoples shall address themselves to the Council of the League of Nations in such a manner as to show the majority of the population of these areas desires independence from Turkey, and if the Council ... recommends that it should be granted to them, Turkey hereby agrees to execute such a recommendation and to renounce all rights and title over these areas.

Wilson's Fourteen Points were the United States' first attempt at a 'new world order' and included honourable demands. Point Five insisted upon:

> a free, open-minded and absolutely impartial adjustment of all colonial claims ... the interests of the populations concerned must have equal weight with the equitable claims of the government whose title is to be determined.

And Point Twelve clearly referred to the Armenians and the Kurds:

> The Turkish portions of the present Ottoman Empire should be assured a secure sovereignty, but the other nationalities which are now under Turkish rule should be assured an undoubted security of life and an absolutely unmolested opportunity of autonomous development ...

Wilson did subsequently award the Armenian republic large areas of modern-day Turkey – including the provinces of Erzerum and Van – but the Turks and the Bolsheviks together destroyed it before the end of December 1920. Unlike a later president, however, Wilson was in no position to send a 'desert storm' and drive out these armies and prevent yet another massacre of Armenians. The Kurds, who had been among the cruellest perpetrators of the Armenian genocide, were equally doomed. Enthusiasm for a British-protected Kurdish state that would act as a buffer between Turkey, Iran and Iraq was extinguished when Britain decided to win over Arab opinion in Iraq by including Kurdish areas in the state and when it became obvious that the emerging Soviet Union might benefit from the creation of a puppet Kurdish state.

American isolationism meant that the Armenians were to be abandoned. The Turks attacked a French army in Cilicia, drove them out of Marash and massacred another fifty thousand Armenians who believed they were living under French protection. A further massacre occurred in Yerevan. Of the Treaty of Lausanne, which registered the final peace between Turkey and the Great Powers, Churchill was to write: 'history will search in vain for the word "Armenia".'

Yet it is important to remember that the one country which – in the immediate aftermath of my father's war – chose a truly democratic alternative to the Middle East was the United States of America. I am not just referring to the Fourteen Points, in themselves a powerful argument for democratic development. In a speech to Congress, Wilson stated that 'people are not to be bartered about from sovereignty to sovereignty as if they were chattels or pawns in a game'. US diplomats and missionaries spread across the old Ottoman empire argued eloquently that the Arabs of the empire should be set up – without Turkey – as one 'modern Arab nation', as they called it, to develop and progress in the world. Another powerful argument came from the King-Crane commission, set up under Wilson, which sailed to the Middle East to actually ask the peoples of the region what they wanted.

It was not Wilson's fault that illness and an increasingly isolationist American public caused a withdrawal from world affairs by the United States. In retrospect, however, that withdrawal – at a time when America was nonpartisan in the Middle East – was one of the great tragedies of our time. We Europeans took over the area. And we failed. When the United States reentered the region a quarter of a century later, it did so for oil and, shortly thereafter, as an almost unquestioning supporter and funder of Israel.

Lord Bryce, whose report on the Armenian genocide had done so much to enlighten public opinion, lamented in a lecture tour of the United States in 1922 that Allied failure to enforce the disarmament of the Turkish army had led the Turks to recover 'their old arrogance'. And in a most enigmatic phrase, he suggested there was more than war-weariness behind the Allied refusal to provide restitution to the Armenians. 'Why the Turkish Government, which had in 1915 massacred a million of its Christian subjects ... why after these crimes that Government should have been treated by the Allies with such extraordinary lenity

– these are mysteries the explanation whereof is probably known to some of you as it is to me,' he said. 'But the secret is one which, as Herodotus says of some of those tales which he heard from the priests in Egypt, is too sacred for me to mention.' The Armenians, Bryce said, had suffered more than any other peoples in the 1914-18 war and had been 'most cruelly abandoned'.

What was the secret of which Bryce claimed privileged knowledge? Was this a mere rhetorical flourish to explain the Allies' postwar irresolution? Or did he think that Britain and France wanted Turkey as an ally in the face of the newly created Bolshevik state that might soon threaten the oilfields of the Middle East? In Transcaucasia, British troops initially opposed the Bolsheviks – 'smelling the oil of Baku', as one observer of the time put it - and for a short time preserved the independence of Georgia, Azerbaijan and a truncated Armenian state. But when Britain withdrew its troops in 1920, the three nations fell to the Soviet Union. In Turkestan, where we were interested in preventing Germany from gaining access to cotton supplies, British forces actually fought the Russians with the assistance of Enver Pasha's Turkish supporters, an odd exchange of alliances, since Tsarist Russia had been an ally of Britain until the 1917 Revolution.

In just one corner of their former Turkish homeland, the Armenians clung on; in the province of Alexandretta and the now broken fortress of Musa Dagh, 20 kilometres west of Antioch, whose people had withstood the siege about which Werfel wrote his novel. Alexandretta fell under French colonial rule in the far north of Syria and so, in 1918, many thousands of Armenians returned to their gutted homes. But to understand this largely forgotten betrayal, the reader must travel to Aanjar, a small town of sorrow that blushes roses around its homes. From the roadside, smothering the front doors, all the way up Father Ashod Karakashian's garden, there is a stream of pink and crimson to mock the suffering of the Armenians who built this town on the malarial marshes of eastern Lebanon in 1939. They are proud people, holders now of Lebanese passports, but holders, too, of one of the darkest secrets of the Armenian past: for they were 'cleansed' from their homeland twice in a century, first in 1915, then in 1939. If they blame the Turks for both evictions, they blame the French as well. And Hitler. Mostly they blame the French.

Father Karakashian's sister Viktoria was just ten in 1939, but she remembers her family's second disaster, a miniature genocide compared to the one in 1915, but nonetheless terrible. 'The French army escorted us all the way,' she said. 'But we were dying. My brother Varoujan was only a year or two old, but I saw him die in my mother's lap in the truck. Like many of us, he had malaria. The French didn't seem to know what to do with us. They took us first for forty days to Abassid in Syria. Then they put us on ships for seven days. We landed at Tripoli [in northern Lebanon] and the French put us on a cattle train to Rayak. From Rayak, they brought us to Aanjar and here we remained.'

Like most of the Armenians of Aanjar, Father Karakashian and his sister were born in Musa Dagh, the Armenian fortress town which is now in south-eastern Turkey and which held out for forty days against overwhelming odds during the genocide. Rescued by French and British warships, the Armenians of Musa Dagh were cared for in Egypt, then sent back to their home town with the French army after the 1914-18 war. And there they lived, in part of the French mandate of Syria, until 1939, when the French government – in a desperate attempt to persuade Turkey to join the Allies against Hitler – 'gave' Musa Dagh and the large city of Alexandretta back to the Turks.

The Karakashian children were born after the 1915 Holocaust, but many of their neighbours have no parents or grandparents. Even when they arrived in Aanjar – which was then in the French mandate of 'Greater Lebanon' – they continued to suffer. 'There were plagues of mosquitoes and this place was a wilderness,' Father Karakashian says. 'The French gave each man 25 Lebanese pounds to break the rocks and build homes for themselves. But many people caught malaria and died.' In the first two years of their ordeal – in 1940, when most of Europe was at war – the Armenians of Aanjar lost a thousand men and women to malaria. Their crumbling gravestones still lie to the north of the town.

The walls of Saint Paul's church in Aanjar are covered with photographs of the Armenian tragedy. One – taken in 1915 – shows the survivors of the Musa Dagh siege climbing desperately onto the deck of an Allied warship. Another shows French officers welcoming Armenian dignitaries back to Alexandretta, along with several men of the French army's 'Armenian Brigade'. In the 1930s, they built a memorial to the siege – it has since been destroyed by the Turks – and when they were forced to leave yet again before the Second World War, the Armenians took their dead, Serb-style, with them. The corpses of eighteen of the 'martyrs' of the 1915 battle – whose bodies had been left untouched by the Turks until the French came with the Armenians in 1918 – were stuffed on to trucks in 1939 together with the refugees, and brought to Aanjar along with the living. They rest now in a marble sarcophagus next to Saint Paul's church. 'In eternal memory,' it says in Armenian on the marble.

But memory has been softened for the people of Aanjar. 'In the first ten years after leaving Alexandretta, the people – there were six thousand deportees who came here – wanted to go back,' Father Karakashian said. 'Then after the Second World War, a lot of our people emigrated to South America. Now we don't want to return. But I went back last year for a holiday. Yes, there is a tiny Armenian community left in our former bit of Turkey around Musa Dagh, thirty families, and they've just renovated the Armenian church. The Turks there are polite to us. I think they know what happened and they respect us because they know they are on our land.'

The shame of France's surrender of the *sanjak* (provincial district) of Alexandretta – including Musa Dagh – is one of the largely untold stories of the Second World War. Fearing that Turkey would join the German Axis as it had in the 1914-18 war, France agreed to a referendum in Alexandretta so that the Armenian and Turkish inhabitants could choose their nationality. The Turks trucked tens of thousands of people into the *sanjak* for the referendum, and naturally the 'people' voted to be part of Turkey. 'The French government made the decision to give the place to Turkey and of course the Armenians realised they couldn't live there any more and requested from the French government that they be taken away and given new homes,' the priest says. 'They wanted to be rid of the Turks. So they left. The French made an agreement in their own interests. I blame the French.' So the *sanjak* of Alexandretta became the Turkish province of Hatay, and the city of Alexandretta became Iskenderun. And the final irony was that Turkey did join the Allied side against Hitler – but only in the last days of the European conflict, when Hitler was about to commit suicide in his Berlin bunker and the Reich was in ashes. The sacrifice of Alexandretta was for nothing.

Nor have its ghosts departed. In 1998, the Turkish prime minister Mesut Yilmaz launched a warning against the Syrians who were assisting the communist Kurdish Workers Party (PKK) guerrillas operating across the border. He chose a ceremony to mark the French handover of Alexandretta to announce that 'those who have their eyes fixed on Turkish territory are suffering from blindness – not even a square centimetre of this country will be taken from it.' Yet Alexandretta had been Armenian. So much for the Treaty of Sèvres.

The world is full of bigger and smaller genocides, some of which we know of from massive testimony and others to which we have blinded ourselves as surely as the Armenian refugee children lost their sight in the vile baths of the refugee homes to which they were taken in 1916. Mark Levene has written extensively about one of the lesser-known genocides – hands up, readers of this book, if you already know of it – when in 1933 the army of the nascent Iraqi state launched an exterminatory attack on members of the Assyrian community. Near the city of Dahuk, the soldiers massacred the entire population of a village called Summayl. The few surviving women were later gang-raped, and Kurds, who formed the predominant ethnic group in the region, joined in the mass killings – in some cases, no doubt, the very same Kurds who had looted and slaughtered the Armenians just across the Turkish border eighteen years earlier. This all happened in British-run Iraq and the local administrative inspector, a Colonel R. S. Stafford, reported to London that Iraqi officers had decided upon the killings with a view to the Assyrians being 'as far as possible ... exterminated'. These Assyrians had been driven from Turkey after genocidal attacks on their villages, had sought sanctuary in Persia, and were then taken by the British to live near Mosul in what would be the new Iraqi state.

Levene has traced this pattern of confrontation with the Iraqi state all the way from 1933 to the Assyrian killings in Saddam's *Anfal* campaign of 1988. But even after the initial massacres, the British stifled an inquiry at the League of Nations by suggesting that it could lead to the collapse of King Feisal's regime, and promptly offered their bombs to the new Iraqi air force for their anti-Assyrian campaign – after the initial killings. The British also warned that a public inquiry might incite 'an outbreak of xenophobia directed at foreigners' – something they only succeeded in doing seventy years later ...

Reprinted by permission of HarperCollins Publishers Ltd
© *Robert Fisk 2005, 2006, with grateful acknowledgements.*

References

1. The Armenians, descended from ancient Urartu, became the first Christian nation when their king Drtad converted from paganism in AD 301, and had to defend their faith against the Persians, who were Zoroastrian before becoming Muslim, and then the Arabs. The Turks arrived from central Asia in the eleventh century. Armenia and Greece were both Christian nations within the Ottoman empire.
2. When Enver held the city of Edirne during the calamitous Balkan wars, thousands of babies were named after the future mass murderer; Enver Hoxha, the mad dictator of Albania, was one, Anwar Sadat, the sane dictator of Egypt, another.
3. The powerful Anglo-Armenian Association lobby group had been founded by Lord Bryce in 1890 and maintained constant pressure on the British government to ensure equal rights for Armenians within the Ottoman Empire. A special supplement to the *Anglo-Armenian Gazette* of April 1895, in the possession of the author, contains a harrowing account of the massacre of Armenians at Sasun, a tub-thumping message of support from Lord Gladstone – 'mere words, coming from the Turk, are not worth the breath spent in uttering them' – and a demand for a European-officered gendarmerie to protect 'Armenian Christians'. Their religion, rather than their minority status in the empire, was clearly the spur to British sentiment.
4. At a conference in Beirut in 2001, Professor Wolfgang Wippermann of the Free University of Berlin introduced evidence that many German officers witnessed the Armenian Massacres without intervening or helping the victims.

⫷OMMUNICATION WORKERS UNION

NO NUCLEAR REPLACEMENT FOR TRIDENT

Billy Hayes
General Secretary

Andy Kerr
President

Where the Bombs Are

Robert S. Norris
Hans M. Kristensen

Robert S. Norris works at the Natural Resources Defense Council and Hans M. Kristensen at the Federation of American Scientists. These excerpts are from their Nuclear Notebook, from the current number of the Bulletin of the Atomic Scientists.

Katharine Lee Bates, the author of 'America the Beautiful', could not have been referring to the expanse of the US nuclear arsenal when she penned the lyric 'from sea to shining sea', but it is fitting. Though it is the smallest it has been since 1958, the US nuclear arsenal continues to sprawl across the country, with thousands of weapons deployed from the coast of Washington State to the coast of Georgia and beyond.

In total, we estimate that the United States deploys and stores nearly 10,000 nuclear weapons at 18 facilities in 12 states and six European countries. The Pentagon developed this extensive network of installations over the past six decades in order to ensure the survivability of its nuclear arsenal. Post-Cold War base closures and arms reductions led to the consolidation of weapons at the current facilities; the number of weapons and their locations will change as the Pentagon implements the June 2004 Nuclear Weapons Stockpile Plan and the 'New Triad'.

Pinpointing the whereabouts of all US nuclear weapons, and especially the numbers stored at specific locations, is fraught with many uncertainties due to the highly classified nature of nuclear weapons information. Declassified documents, leaks, official statements, news reports, and conversations with current and former officials provide many clues, as do high-resolution satellite images of many of these facilities. Such images are available to anyone with a computer and internet access, thanks to Google Earth and commercial satellite imaging companies such as DigitalGlobe. This development introduces important new tools for research and advances citizen verification. The statistics contained in this article represent our best estimates, based on many years of closely following nuclear issues.

The nuclear weapons network shrank during the past decade, with the Pentagon removing nuclear weapons from three states (California,

Virginia, and South Dakota) and the size of the stockpile decreasing from about 12,500 warheads to nearly 10,000. Consolidation slowed considerably compared with the period between 1992 and 1997, when the Pentagon withdrew nuclear weapons from 10 states and several European bases, and the total stockpile decreased from 18,290 to 12,500 warheads.

Approximately 62 per cent of the current stockpile belongs to the air force and is stored at seven bases in the United States and eight bases in six European countries; the navy stores its weapons at two submarine bases, one on each coast. None of the other services possesses nuclear weapons.

The ballistic missile submarine base at Bangor, Washington, contains nearly 24 per cent of the entire stockpile, or some 2,364 warheads, the largest contingent. The Bangor installation is home to a majority (nine) of the navy's nuclear-powered ballistic missile submarines and a large number of surplus W76 warheads that will eventually be retired and disassembled. Its counterpart on the Atlantic coast, Kings Bay Submarine Base in Georgia, is the third-largest contingent, with some 1,364 warheads. Each base stores approximately 150 nuclear sea-launched cruise missiles.

Minot Air Force Base (AFB) in North Dakota, with more than 800 bombs and cruise missiles for its B-52 bombers and more than 400 warheads for its Minuteman III intercontinental ballistic missile wing, has the largest number of active air force weapons. The other B-52 wing at Barksdale Air Force Base in Louisiana has more than 900 warheads, and Whiteman Air Force Base in Missouri has more than 130 bombs for its B-2 bombers.

The large underground facility at Kirtland Air Force Base in Albuquerque, New Mexico, stores more than 1,900 warheads that are either part of the inactive/reserve stockpile or awaiting shipment across Interstate 40 to the Pantex Plant outside of Amarillo, Texas, for dismantlement. The 970-acre facility at Nellis Air Force Base, Nevada, north-east of Las Vegas, performs a similar function, storing approximately 900 warheads in 75 igloos – 'one of the largest stockpiles in the free world', according to the air force.

During the Cold War, the United States deployed a large percentage (up to one-third) of its nuclear weapons in other countries and at sea. At its peak arsenal size in the late 1960s, the United States stored weapons in 17 different countries. By the mid-1980s, there were about 14,000 weapons in 26 US states, 6,000 more at overseas US and NATO bases, and another 4,000 on ships at sea.

The United States terminated many nuclear missions after the end of the Cold War and retired the weapons. It withdrew all of its nuclear weapons from South Korea in 1991 and thousands more from Europe by 1993. The army and Marine Corps denuclearised in the early 1990s, and in 1992 the navy swiftly off-loaded all nuclear weapons from aircraft carriers and other surface vessels. By 1994, the navy had eliminated these ships' nuclear capability, and many air force, navy, and army bases and storage depots closed overseas as a result. Today, perhaps as many as 400 bombs remain at eight facilities in six European countries, the last remnant of a bygone era.

Nuclear weapons: A disarmament deficit

Hans Blix

In November 2006, Dr Blix spoke to the British Institute of International and Comparative Law about his 'Reflections on the Opinion of the International Court of Justice on the Legality of the Threat or Use of Nuclear Weapons'. He is currently Chairman of the Commission on Weapons of Mass Destruction.

In July this year it was 10 years since the International Court of Justice rendered its *Advisory Opinion on the Legality of the Threat or Use of Nuclear Weapons*. This is also the year of another anniversary in the efforts to rid the world of nuclear weapons. It was 60 years ago that the General Assembly declared its determination to physically eliminate 'atomic weapons' and other weapons of mass destruction. While that declared determination has resulted in two comprehensive conventions outlawing biological and chemical weapons, it has not borne fruit as regards nuclear weapons. Many would question whether any nuclear weapon states – except South Africa – have yet seriously pursued the idea.

I do not propose to examine the many important legal questions which the Advisory Opinion examines. Others are doing this with admirable scholarship. Having spent much time in operational and diplomatic work on arms control and disarmament I think it may be more interesting for me to comment on the current political and legal landscape in the field of non-use of force, arms control, nuclear disarmament and non-proliferation of nuclear weapons against the background of positions taken by the Court.

My discussion will focus on four matters:
● The context of international relations in which the opinion was given;
● The UN Charter restrictions on the threat or use of force;
● The fragmented approach that has been taken and continues to be taken by the world community to eliminate nuclear weapons; and
● The deficit in implementation of article VI of the Non-Proliferation Treaty (NPT), requiring negotiations toward nuclear disarmament.

During the last three years I have had the honour to chair an Independent International Commission on Weapons of Mass Destruction and on 1 June this year the fourteen member Commission presented a unanimously adopted report with the title *Weapons of Terror: Freeing the World of Nuclear, Biological and Chemical Arms* (see *Spokesman 92*). It contains 60 recommendations, 30 of them having regard to nuclear weapons. I shall try to relate some of the report's thoughts on the reduction of the threats posed by nuclear weapons to the findings of the Court.

In 1994, the General Assembly of the United Nations asked the International Court of Justice: 'Is the threat or use of nuclear weapons in any circumstances permitted under international law?'

In its advisory opinion the Court unanimously held that:

'A threat or use of force by means of nuclear weapons that is contrary to Article 2, paragraph 4, of the United Nations Charter and that fails to meet all the requirements of Article 51 is unlawful.'

And:

'A threat or use of nuclear weapons should also be compatible with the requirements of the international law applicable in armed conflict, particularly those of the principles and rules of international humanitarian law, as well as with specific obligations under treaties and other undertakings which expressly deal with nuclear weapons.'

Further, in a part of the Opinion, which was adopted through the President's casting vote, the Court declared that while the threat or use of nuclear weapons would generally be contrary to the rules of international law, it was not possible to reach a definite conclusion regarding the legality, or illegality, of the use of nuclear weapons by a state 'in an extreme circumstance of self-defence, in which its very survival would be at stake'.

Obviously this conclusion, although leaving only an uncertain and narrow window for a possible legal use of a nuclear weapon, went against the argument that the cumulated effect of a number of existing rules of international law, such as those prohibiting indiscriminate weapons or weapons causing unnecessary suffering, would be a categorical ban on the use of nuclear weapons. As had been argued by *inter alia* the United Kingdom in a written statement presented to the Court, a low yield nuclear weapon could conceivably be used 'against warships on the High Seas or troops in sparsely populated areas', in which case the civilian casualties would be as limited as when conventional weapons are used.

The language chosen by the majority of the Court in this part can be, and has been, criticised. It may seem, as Judge Schwebel points out in his Dissenting Opinion, that the legal conclusion to be drawn from the reasoning is that the use of nuclear weapons is permitted, unless the action is rendered illegal under international law in the specific circumstances under which the weapon is used.

Nevertheless, although the Court did not find any absolute prohibition in international conventional or customary law against the threat or use of nuclear weapons, it wanted and did convey the sense that in most circumstances the use of a nuclear weapon would collide with some rule of international law. I do not see that anything has happened since 1996 that would encourage a bolder view of the legal situation.

This brings me to the first of the four matters which I referred to – the temporary context in which the Opinion was delivered.

The temporary context of the opinion – and the situation today

Ten years ago, multilateral efforts towards nuclear disarmament, compared to those made today, were relatively successful:

- A nuclear weapons programme in Iraq had been uprooted;
- Activities in North Korea to produce plutonium through reprocessing had been stopped, following an understanding reached with the United States;
- Chemical weapons had been completely outlawed through a convention, after decades of negotiation;
- A treaty comprehensively prohibiting nuclear weapons tests had been concluded;
- The Non-Proliferation Treaty had just been extended indefinitely; and
- The nuclear weapon states parties to the treaty had made significant and specific commitments in fulfilment of their obligations under article VI of the NPT.

Throughout the reasoning in the Advisory Opinion of the Court there is – understandably against this background of progress – an innuendo of a categorical ban around the corner. The Court refers to an 'increasing concern' about nuclear weapons in the international community, and that this could be seen as a 'foreshadowing of a future general prohibition of the use of such weapons'.

If the idea of a general prohibition of use was ever on the minds of nuclear weapon states, it must have faded fast and is certainly not there today. The horror vision of the nuclear weapons also faded in the public mind.

It may seem paradoxical that the international community, after the end of the Cold War, in an era with no major ideological differences between great powers, was unable to agree on new measures to address the threats posed by weapons of mass destruction (WMD). Sadly, we must note, however, that the world's governments missed the opportunity to move to disarmament.

Despite some valuable progress in arms control and disarmament during the 1990s – *inter alia* bringing the number of nuclear weapons down from over 50,000 to some 27,000 through elimination of excess – we are actually in a phase of rearmament. Last year the world spent about one trillion dollars on military expenses and we do not discuss this much.

The commitments to further arms control disarmament measures made by the nuclear weapon states in 1995, when the non-nuclear weapon states accepted to extend the treaty and their pledges indefinitely, are being ignored. For instance, the Comprehensive Test Ban Treaty, which was concluded in 1996 after decades of negotiations, has been left in limbo – and will remain so unless the United States and China and some other states ratify it.

The 2005 Review Conference of the Non-Proliferation Treaty ended in bitterness with many non-nuclear weapon states feeling cheated. The World Summit at the UN in September 2005 was unable to agree on a single line regarding arms control, disarmament or non-proliferation, and the Geneva

Conference on Disarmament has been unable for about a decade to agree on a work programme.

Today, the world's attention is focused on North Korea's missiles and testing of a plutonium bomb and the development by Iran of a uranium enrichment capability, which could be used at some future date to produce highly enriched uranium for bombs. We also hear concerns that terrorists might acquire nuclear weapons or at least 'dirty bombs' – i.e. bombs containing radioactive material.

All this focusing on non-proliferation and terrorism is justified. It should not, however, lead us to ignore some unwelcome realities. It is true that nuclear weapons may be particularly dangerous in some hands, but they are dangerous in anybody's hands. There are still some 27,000 nuclear weapons in the world –most of them in the United States and Russia. Large numbers of these weapons are on hair trigger alert and we hear again and again from Washington that 'all options are on the table'.

Sadly, the general prohibition of use of nuclear weapons foreshadowed by the International Court of Justice has not materialised. Rather we have been witnessing not only a stagnation in the sphere of arms control and disarmament, and some rearmament, but also an attribution of greater importance to nuclear weapons and interest in their development:

● Several nuclear weapon states no longer give pledges against a first use of nuclear weapons;

● The development of a missile shield in the United States is perceived by China and Russia as a step potentially allowing the US to threaten them with nuclear weapons while creating immunity for the US; they are taking steps to meet this perceived threat;

● The development and testing of new types of nuclear weapons is urged by influential groups in the US; in the United Kingdom many expect a government decision about a renewal of the nuclear weapons programme, stretching it far beyond 2020;

● The stationing of weapons in space is considered in the US; if it were to occur, other states might follow and threats may arise to the world's peaceful uses of space and the enormous investments made in them.

Not surprisingly against this background the central message in the Report of the Weapons of Mass Destruction Commission is that the arms control and disarmament process must be revived and pursued in parallel with non-proliferation efforts aimed at preventing the spread of weapons of mass destruction to further states and to terrorist movements.

I now come to the second matter on which I want to focus: the general prohibition of the threat or use of force as a means of eliminating the threat of nuclear weapons

The Court rejected various conventions on the protection of the environment, the Genocide Convention of 1948, and human rights instruments as grounds for a general and absolute prohibition of the use of nuclear weapons. The central provisions were seen rather to be the restrictions on the threat or use of force in article 2:4 of the UN Charter, the two exceptions to this norm, and the norms and principles of international humanitarian law.

The two exceptions to the prohibition of the threat or use of force in article 2:4 of the UN Charter are found in:

● Article 51, which preserves a right to individual and collective self-defence, when an armed attack occurs, until the Security Council has taken the necessary measures; and

● Article 42, which allows the Security Council to intervene under Chapter VII – if need by authorising military force – to stop 'threats to the peace, breaches of the peace or acts of aggression'.

The Court did not find it necessary, on the basis of the statements presented before it, to address questions that might arise from the application of Chapter VII. Did it consider it out of question that the Council might authorise a use of nuclear weapons?

In declaring that it is not possible to conclude that the use of nuclear weapons would be illegal in all possible cases, the Court relies on the reserved right to exercise individual or collective self-defence. In this context, the Court cites its own judgement in the *Nicaragua Case (1986)*, declaring that self-defence must be carried out in a manner respecting the dual principles of 'necessity' and 'proportionality'. The Court also highlights the requirement that all acts of war to be consistent with applicable norms of International Humanitarian Law. The Court notes that in most instances the use of nuclear weapons would not fulfil all of these requirements, but it does not go into a detailed discussion on smaller tactical nuclear weapons with more limited effects, or on specific circumstances under which the use of nuclear weapons would be permitted in the exercise of self-defence. Instead the Court simply states:

> '[I]t suffices for the Court to note that the very nature of all nuclear weapons and the profound risks associated therewith are further considerations to be borne in mind by States believing they can exercise a nuclear response in self-defence in accordance with the requirements of proportionality.'

The statement holds great significance at a time when nuclear weapons have regained a central position in the defence strategies and doctrines of the nuclear weapon states and when article 51 of the Charter may be ignored by various states through the application of a doctrine of preventive and pre-emptive self-defence.

Pre-emptive and preventive use of force

In 2003, the war in Iraq was launched by a number of states without the authorisation of the Security Council. Indeed, they were perfectly aware that their action would not obtain an authorisation of the Council.

The United States did not officially argue that the war was justified as a preventive or pre-emptive action against an Iraqi threat of attack, but there is no doubt that this view was held. A US National Security Strategy had been published in September 2002. It stated flatly that a limitation of the right unilaterally to use armed force in self-defence to cases where 'armed attacks' were occurring or were 'imminent' would be insufficient in the era of missiles and terrorists. That was tantamount to saying that UN Charter Article 51 might be ignored.

The position taken in 2002 by the US was confirmed in the National Security Strategy of 2006 and many statements by the US President and other officials threatening armed action against any 'growing threat' and declaring in the cases of Iran and North Korea that 'all options are on the table'.

One must conclude that the current US administration asserts the freedom – at least for itself – to use force, with the weapons it chooses, without any authorisation by the Security Council, even if there is no armed attack, ongoing or imminent. A statement by the current US ambassador to the UN confirms that in his view restrictions in the UN Charter on the use of force are simply not relevant to the US. He said:

'Our actions, taken consistently with Constitutional principles, require no separate, external validation to make them legitimate ...' (2003)

While the overwhelming majority of states reject the US claims to such a wide licence on the use of armed force, there may be a risk that these US policies and doctrines, the development of smaller nuclear weapons and a trend towards the 'conventionalisation' of such weapons could, one day, lead to the use of nuclear weapons. The Weapons of Mass Destruction Commission urges a return to respect for the UN Charter provisions on the use of force.

I come to the third matter on which I want to focus: the fragmented approach which governments have taken to restrict the deployment and prohibit or restrict the use of nuclear weapons

The most effective way to prevent the use of nuclear weapons would be to eliminate the weapons themselves. The physical elimination of nuclear weapons would give greater confidence about non-use than a mere prohibition of use. If there are no weapons there will be no use. Such elimination could be achieved through a comprehensive – and verified – ban on production, acquisition and stockpiling.

While the Commission pleads for the goal of a convention 'outlawing' nuclear weapons in a way similar to what has been done regarding biological and chemical weapons, it also realises the short and medium term obstacles to attaining such a convention. It notes, as the Court does, that governments have taken a fragmentary approach to the elimination of use and production of nuclear weapons. Thus, they have taken steps

- to ban the deployment of nuclear weapons in various environments (the Antarctic, the sea-bed and outer space);
- to impede a qualitative development of the nuclear weapons by treaty bans on testing;
- to limit the possession of the weapons through commitments under treaties establishing nuclear-weapon-free zones; all countries in the Southern hemisphere are covered by such zones;
- to limit the possession of nuclear weapons through commitments under the Non-Proliferation Treaty; and
- to oblige the nuclear weapon states parties to the NPT to pursue negotiations in good faith on nuclear disarmament;

● to commit the nuclear weapon states – on various conditions and with various reservations – not to use nuclear weapons against non-nuclear weapon states;

Implementation of Article 6 of the NPT

The fourth and last matter I want to focus on in relation to the Advisory Opinion has regard to the concern expressed by the Court about the lack of implementation of article VI of the Non-Proliferation Treaty. While this matter did not form a part of the question put before the Court by the General Assembly, it can hardly be ignored.

The Treaty is seen as a double bargain aiming at a world free of nuclear weapons:

● the non-nuclear weapons states parties commit themselves in Article II not to acquire the weapons; and

● the nuclear weapons states parties commit themselves in Article VI to negotiate toward nuclear disarmament.

We often hear warnings that this double bargain risks collapse because of violations by some states which have joined as non-nuclear. While readily recognising that the Treaty is under strain, the Weapons of Mass Destruction Commission notes that the world is not full of would-be violators and that the overwhelming commitment to the Treaty remains of tremendous value.

Without the Non-Proliferation Treaty nuclear weapons might have spread to many more than the eight or nine states which now have them. However, the treaty and the fundamental bargain are under strain today. Iraq, Libya and North Korea ignored their non-proliferation pledges under Article II, Iran is under suspicion to do the same; and the five nuclear weapon states parties are not living up to their pledges under Article VI to move to nuclear disarmament.

Among non-nuclear weapon states parties there is a strong feeling of frustration, even of being cheated by the nuclear weapon states parties, for instance, when the have-states are in the process of deciding the development of new types of weapons rather than examining how they could manage their defence needs with other weapons than nuclear.

The negotiations with North Korea and Iran would not be easy under any circumstance, but they might be somewhat less difficult if the nuclear weapon states participating could show that they themselves were actively striving for and leading the world toward nuclear disarmament. Such action would respond to the International Court of Justices's demand for the pursuit in good faith negotiations – not for the mere sake of negotiations but – to achieve precise results.

The Weapons of Mass Destruction Commission therefore submits – in its very first recommendation – that all parties to the Treaty need 'revert to the fundamental and balanced non-proliferation and disarmament commitments that were made under the Treaty and confirmed in 1995 when the Treaty was extended indefinitely'.

Let me now conclude by noting some of the specific recommendations of the Commission, starting with some important organisational items:

● Given the setbacks in arms control and disarmament, notably at the UN summit in 2005 and the continued stalemate, there is a need to give new impetus. The Commission suggests that the General Assembly should convene a World Summit on disarmament, non-proliferation and terrorist use of weapons of mass destruction. Thorough preparations would be necessary and planning should start as soon as possible. (Recommendation 59)

● The Conference on Disarmament in Geneva, the principal international forum for negotiation on weapons-of-mass-destruction-related issues, has been unable to adopt a programme of work for almost a decade. The Commission suggests that the Conference should be able to adopt a programme of work, by a qualified majority of two-thirds. (Recommendation 58).

● The Commission report suggests that the Security Council should establish a small subsidiary unit that could provide professional technical information and advice on matters relating to weapons of mass destruction. (Recommendation 56) Such independent advice would have been of interest on the question of the nature of the test explosion in North Korea.

● The Non-Proliferation Treaty should be given a standing secretariat. (Recommendation 4).

I continue with a number of the substantive measures that the Commission recommends:

● No measure could be more urgent, important in substance and as a signal that arms control and disarmament are again on the world agenda than signature and ratification of the Comprehensive Nuclear-Test-Ban Treaty by states which have not yet done so. (Recommendation 28). If the Treaty were seen to lapse, there would be an increased risk that some state might restart weapons tests. Demanding in negotiations with North Korea that the country should deposit its ratification of the Treaty – which is necessary for the Treaty to enter into force – would be easier if all the states participating in the six power talks had, themselves, ratified the Treaty.

● Negotiating without further delay a treaty prohibiting the production of fissile material for weapons (FMCT) is the next most urgent issue to tackle. (Recommendation 26). The combination of a continued reduction in the number of existing nuclear weapons and a verified closing of the tap for more weapons fissile material would gradually reduce the world inventory of bombs. A draft of a cut-off treaty has been presented in Geneva. It has important weaknesses but should be discussed.

● The Commission is of the view that such a treaty prohibiting the production of fissile material for weapons, to be meaningful, must provide for effective international verification of all enrichment and reprocessing activities. Independent international verification is already carried out by EURATOM in enrichment plants in two nuclear weapon states – France and the United Kingdom. Enrichment plants in Brazil and Japan are subject to International Atomic Energy Agency safeguards verification. If there is no effective international verification, any controversy about respect for the treaty would have to be discussed on the basis of evidence coming only from national means of verification. We know from the case of Iraq that this would not be satisfactory. Moreover, without independent verification suspicions about violations might arise and lead to a race between some countries in the production of fissile material.

● Further steps, by all nuclear weapon states, towards reducing strategic nuclear arsenals would be significant. The Commission recommends that the United States and Russia, which have the most weapons, should take the lead. With increasing cooperation between Russia and the European Union, Russian nuclear weapons should be withdrawn from forward deployment to central storage and US nuclear weapons should be withdrawn to US territory. (Recommendations 20, 21 and 22).

● In the view of the Commission all states that have nuclear weapons should commit themselves categorically to a policy of no first use (Recommendation 15) and the US and Russia should reciprocally take their nuclear weapons off hair trigger alert. (Recommendation 17).

● As the reliance on nuclear power is expected to go up, the need for a greater production of low enriched uranium fuel, and for the disposal of spent fuel, can be anticipated. This must occur in a manner that does not increase the risk of diversion of material and the risk of proliferation. The International Atomic Energy Agency should be the forum for such exploration. (Recommendation 8).

● Regional approaches should also be further developed, especially in sensitive areas. It would, for example, be desirable to obtain commitments from the states on the Korean peninsula and in the Middle East (including Iran and Israel) that they would accept a verified suspension for a prolonged period of time of any production of enriched uranium and plutonium while obtaining international assurances of the supply of fuel for any civilian nuclear power. (Recommendation 12)

● Lastly, you will not be surprised to hear me submit that international professional inspection, such as it has been practised under the UN, the International Atomic Energy Agency and the Chemical Weapons Convention, is an important and economic tool for verification. Such inspection does not stand in any contradiction to national means of verification. Rather these two means of fact-finding supplement each other. Many states have no national means that they can use and should not have to be dependent upon the intelligence of other states. States which operate intelligence may, in one-way traffic arrangements, provide information to the international verification systems. (Recommendation 55).

● The safeguards system of the International Atomic Energy Agency needs to be strengthened through a universal acceptance of the additional protocol. (Recommendation 3). The effective operation of the safeguards system should never have to suffer for financial reasons. It is paradoxical for the world community to spend billions on inspections to ensure that no material or equipment of nuclear relevance is transported in containers or baggage in air travel and to deny the safeguards system the fullest support.

These are some of the suggestions put forward by the Weapons of Mass Destruction Commission. Even though the world might not within the next ten years attain a comprehensive convention against the use, production or acquisition of nuclear weapons, acting upon the recommendations would be important to take us in the direction of a nuclear-weapon-free world.

Woe unto Trident

Alan McDonald

The Moderator of the General Assembly of the Church of Scotland, the Right Reverend Alan McDonald, reports here on a visit to Aldermaston.

On 12 June 2006, I joined a delegation from Scotland which went to the Atomic Weapons Establishment at Aldermaston. The visit was organised by Scottish CND. The delegation consisted of Members of the Scottish Parliament, together with religious, trades union and others leaders from Scottish civic society. The purpose of the visit was to inspect the establishment at Aldermaston, and see for ourselves what is being done there, in our name. I agreed to be part of the delegation because I thought it was a creative contribution to the debate about nuclear weapons in this country.

There had been a tendency of late, at least until when Gordon Brown made a speech, that the debate about Trident had almost become confined to set piece demonstrations at Faslane. I was encouraged that CND were taking a new initiative, and approaching the issue of Trident from a slightly new direction. After all, the Prime Minister, Tony Blair, has said that he wants there to be 'an open public debate' about the possible replacement for the Trident ballistic missile system. It is hard to have a meaningful debate without being in possession of all the facts. It is also the case that Governments have argued for years that while what happens in Aldermaston is of a sensitive nature, the purpose of the establishment is not a secret and there is nothing to hide. The delegation from Scotland went in expectation, but sadly we were turned away at the front gate of Aldermaston. We sent a letter of protest to the Secretary of State for Defence, and I was at least allowed, along with Robin Harper MSP, to briefly go inside Aldermaston to hand in a copy of the letter.

Local groups which have been monitoring developments at Aldermaston over the years then took us for their 'alternative' tour of the base, stopping at various points around the perimeter fence to point out the extent of the establishment, but also the preparations for new developments. As we made our way round the miles of perimeter fence, we were shown the probable site for one of the world's most powerful supercomputers, a Cray XT3, costing £20 million. The computer will be able to simulate in great detail the detonation of a nuclear weapon. The computer, to be known as Larch, will be so fast, that, as the Systems Manager at Aldermaston puts it 'The 6 billion inhabitants of earth would each have to make nearly 7,000 calculations per second to keep up with it.' However, for followers of the crucified and risen Christ there is a much more telling calculation — precisely how obscene is it to spend £20 million to simulate a nuclear weapon when so many of the 6 billion inhabitants of earth still exist on less than a dollar a day?

After our visit to Aldermaston, the delegation from Scotland was taken to Westminster for a session of a Commons Select Committee. The Committee had gathered to take evidence from Dr Hans Blix, the former nuclear weapons inspector in Iraq. We met Dr Blix, who was presenting the eagerly awaited report of the Weapons of Mass Destruction Commission: *Weapons of Terror – Freeing the World of Nuclear, Biological and Chemical Arms* [see *Spokesman 92*]. The Commission makes 60 recommendations, one of which, number 23, seems to have particular relevance for the United Kingdom at this time. 'Any state contemplating replacement or modernisation of its nuclear weapon systems must consider such action in the light of all relevant treaty obligations and its duty to contribute to the nuclear disarmament process. As a minimum, it must refrain from developing nuclear weapons with new military capabilities or for new missions. It must not adopt systems or doctrines that blur the distinction between nuclear and conventional weapons or lower the nuclear threshold.'

Back at Aldermaston, we were shown the site of a new laser system which would be critical in the design of any new thermonuclear weapon. And finally, we stood outside the fence and looked at the site for the new A90 building which will manufacture plutonium parts for nuclear weapons.

In July 2005, when he was Secretary of State for Defence, John Reid announced a three year investment of over £1 billion for the Atomic Weapons Establishment at Aldermaston. Included in that figure was the construction of the new supercomputer, and the new highly powered laser system. What is not clear, is whether this massive sum of money would be included in the figure of £25 Billion, for the cost of a replacement for Trident. Most commentators think this is additional spending to the estimated figure of £25 billion, making that figure even more obscene. And talking of obscene – let's just remind ourselves what we're talking about.

On 6 August 1945, the United States Air Force dropped an atomic bomb on the Japanese city of Hiroshima. Three days later a second atomic bomb was dropped on the city of Nagasaki. At least 100,000 people died almost immediately in these cities as a result of two bombs. The atomic bomb which was used at Hiroshima was equivalent to 13,000 tons of TNT. The bomb used at Nagasaki was equivalent to 20,000 tons of TNT.

The statistics about Trident are chilling. There are four Trident nuclear submarines based at Faslane, just up the road from Glasgow. Each submarine can carry 16 missiles. Each missile can be armed with up to 12 nuclear warheads with a range of 6,000 miles. One Trident submarine can carry the equivalent of 750

Hiroshima atom bombs. The potential for the indiscriminate destruction of countless men, women and children is almost beyond belief. The threat to the future of creation is beyond imagining.

For me, how we respond to the issue of nuclear weapons is close to the heart of what it means to be a Christian today. It is very important for me as a minister of the Church of Scotland to acknowledge that, since 1981, the General Assembly has, through many deliverances, adopted a very clear position on this issue. The Assembly has said, along with every other mainstream church, that nuclear weapons and weapons of mass destruction are morally and theologically wrong.

Luke, chapter 6, verses 17 to 26 is one of the most important sermons Jesus ever preached, and includes the Beatitudes, sometimes called the heart of the Gospel. And the message that Jesus preaches turns the world upside down. The message says: 'Blessed … are you poor, the kingdom of God is yours. Blessed … are you who are hungry now, you will be filled. Blessed … are you who weep now, you will laugh …' The listeners to this Sermon in Luke would have been astonished because this was not their experience of poverty, hunger, and tears. And neither is it our experience today. The Beatitudes are as sharp and relevant as they were 2000 years ago. This message of Jesus challenges all our assumptions about what life is for. But Luke goes on to add some verses that we don't find in Matthew's version of the Beatitudes. In some translations these are known as the 'Woes', for they literally say 'Woe to you'. In the Good News translation of the Bible the text says 'How Terrible': 'How terrible for you who are rich now, you have had your easy life … How terrible for you who are full now, you will go hungry … How terrible for you who laugh now, you will mourn and weep …' And once again those listening must have been astonished, for this was not their experience of riches, and security, and laughter. And neither is it our experience today. This message of Jesus challenges all our expectations and assumptions about life. These words of Jesus are hard, but not threatening words. These are words of concern and compassion. Jesus is telling us that if our heart's desire is only 'me, my and mine', then ultimately it will not bring happiness or fulfilment.

This is a serious challenge to the way of the world, which tells us, 'to get, to have, to consume, to look after number one, to keep to ourselves, to defend what we have'. But the message at the heart of the gospel is that if we only think about me, then ultimately it will affect not only me, but also our sisters and brothers in this global village, and the intricate web of creation which we inhabit together. It is no coincidence that, in the verses that follow the Beatitudes in the Gospel of Luke, Jesus speaks about loving our enemies. The Beatitudes represent the very heart of the Gospel of Jesus Christ. Nuclear weapons represent the reverse of the Gospel — the indiscriminate threat to incinerate men, women, and children, and threaten the future of creation.

Our Christian faith teaches us that we are not powerless in the struggle to preach the gospel about the love of God. We can make a difference in the world. Each one of us must decide the most faithful way of living our daily lives as disciples of Jesus Christ.

When this meeting was first planned, we wondered if anyone would be interested in whether there was life after Trident. Then the Chancellor of the Exchequer made a speech at the Mansion House. And yesterday, in Scotland, in the church where his father was a Church of Scotland minister, Gordon Brown said he was sure his late father would have agreed with him about nuclear weapons. Well who knows, but we do know that the Church of Scotland has opposed nuclear weapons for the past 25 years. The Chancellor is due great credit for his part in the Make Poverty History campaign. However, what is the point of making poverty history if you then effectively target the poor, and everybody else in the world, with nuclear weapons? And there is a crucial question in this debate which perhaps can best be answered for us only by the Chancellor of the Exchequer: How much aid for the developing world could you buy with £25 billion? How many lives could be saved?

But even if a Trident replacement cost nothing, even if the system came free from the land of George W Bush, we should still have nothing to do with it. Because it's wrong, morally, and theologically wrong. There has been some discussion lately, in this Post-Cold-War, new War-on-Terrorism World, about exactly who we would target with our new, improved nuclear weapons? And that is indeed a good question that brings out the insanity of nuclear weapons today. But for Christians, as people who believe in the resurrection, the answer to that question about who we point these missiles at is, the target would be Jesus Christ, the Son of God, along with millions of his brothers and sisters. For people of faith this is no way to love our neighbour. For people who believe in the Creator God, 'Son of Trident' is not the way to care for this beautiful world or to hand it on to our children and our children's children. Let us not replace Trident. Just don't do it!

Blessed are the Peacemakers

Cardinal Keith O'Brien

Cardinal O'Brien is President of the Bishops' Conference of Scotland. Here he rejects any arms race, above all the nuclear one.

You are aware of the cause which brings us together. It is the invitation to enter into debate requested by our Prime Minister, Mr Tony Blair, regarding the possible renewal of the Trident Nuclear Weapons System. Chancellor Gordon Brown has given added urgency to this debate at this time, following on his own statement.

In my own presentation this evening, I intend to do two things: give some indication of the history of my own involvement in this issue; and give something of my Church's teaching with regard to nuclear deterrence.

Like any good Christian, the call to peace was quite simply basic to my call as a Christian. Aware of many Old Testament readings regarding 'beating swords into ploughshares' and texts like that, I saw the teaching of Jesus Christ as a natural continuation of the desire for peace among the people of the Old Testament, despite wars and conflicts which surrounded them.

Obviously, Christ himself was the great peacemaker. Peace and reconciliation was always an underlying theme in his teaching and we remember those very beautiful words of the Sermon on the Mount: 'Blessed are the peacemakers for they shall be called children of God!'.

'We try to realise as Christians that we are sisters and brothers and that the earth is our common inheritance. We have a responsibility to share this world with everyone else, to pass it on uncontaminated, unpillaged, unspoiled, to future generations. We have to rid ourselves of prejudice and mutual suspicion. We must totally reject any "arms race", any policy of revengeful slaughter, all greed and self-preservation at the expense of others.' And there I quote a statement from my own Bishops' Conference issued in 1982.

In that statement of 1982, the members of the Roman Catholic Bishops' Conference of Scotland stated with regard to nuclear weapons: 'We are convinced that if it is immoral to use these weapons, it is also immoral to threaten their use. Some argue that the threat can be justified as the lesser of two evils. The crux of the problem is whether in any foreseeable circumstance a policy of self-defence based on the use or even the threat of use of these weapons of terrible destructiveness can ever be morally justified'.

Those words 'if it is immoral to use these weapons, it is also immoral to threaten their use' caused me to think deeply on this issue some 20 years ago.

Having that statement before us, the members of the present Bishops' Conference of Scotland issued a statement regarding the possibility of the Trident replacement on 11 April 2006. We welcomed the Prime Minister's comment that there should be the fullest possible public debate on the Trident Nuclear Missile System. And we stated then that: 'We urge the Government of the United Kingdom not to invest in a replacement for the Trident System and to begin the process of decommissioning these weapons with the intention of diverting the sums spent on nuclear weaponry to programmes of aid and development'.

I myself developed my own thought in my Easter Sunday sermon on Sunday 16 April 2006, indicating that as Easter people we must not only be people of prayer, but people of action, living in that Easter promise of peace from Jesus himself, whose first words after his Resurrection were: 'Peace be with you'.

In that letter I spoke of the consistent teaching of the Church on war, especially nuclear war – to which I will refer later.

I indicated that: 'We here in Britain are in a marvellous position to take concrete steps towards making real the demand of Pope Benedict XVI in his New Year message (see *Spokesman 90*) for peace when he stated with regard to nuclear arms as a means of ensuring security in their countries that "This point of view is not only baneful but also completely fallacious. In a nuclear war there would be no victors, only victims".' I added that here in Scotland we have a duty to lead the way in campaigning for change because we have the shameful responsibility of housing these horrific weapons. And I called on my own people to demand that these weapons of mass destruction be replaced, but not with more weapons of mass destruction. Rather, I asked that Trident be replaced with projects that bring life to the poor!

On 15 May, I led representatives of the principal Churches here in Scotland in the signing of a petition on the replacement of Trident nuclear weapons outside the Scottish Parliament. The petition reads: 'We the undersigned urge the Government of the United Kingdom not to invest in a replacement for the Trident System and to begin now the process of decommissioning these weapons with the intention of diverting the sums spent on nuclear weaponry to programmes of aid and development'. Copies of that national petition are available at this meeting and I do urge you to sign them and to bring them back to your own communities and towns.

In my own Archdiocese, I launched a process of education on the whole matter of 'Nuclear Weapons and Catholic Teaching' – with study evenings being organised throughout my Archdiocese. As a follow-up to this, our own Church's

National Commission for Justice and Peace are making copies of this study evening, which is available in a power point presentation to all those who request it, as a means for further education of people throughout the length and breadth of Scotland.

In what I have said above, I have indicated something of the position of the Roman Catholic Church with regard to war in general and hinted at the position which I believe is now the firm teaching of the Church.

Over the centuries there have been various theories with regard to war and its justification. With regard to nuclear deterrence, we might say that the Catholic Church has moved along a line from reluctant acceptance of nuclear deterrence to a firm position against any form of deterrence – this progression having taken place over the past 40 years and being consistent in as much as it always has sought disarmament.

In a 1982 UN address, Pope John Paul II said: 'In current conditions [ie, in 1982] deterrence based on balance certainly not as an end in itself but as a step on the way toward a progressive disarmament, may still be judged morally acceptable'. And he added the crucial next sentence: 'Nonetheless in order to ensure peace, it is indispensable not to be satisfied with this minimum which is always susceptible to the real danger of explosion'. Pope John Paul was referring to conditions in 1982, and they did not improve much throughout that whole decade.

By the 1990s it was becoming increasingly clear that the biggest nuclear powers had no intention of negotiating the removal of nuclear weapons, nor did they intend to disarm. Belief in the goodwill of the nuclear powers had been the mainstay of the Holy See's reluctant acceptance of temporary nuclear deterrence. It had also realised, what it seems that nuclear nations have yet to realise, that the world is a very different place in the 21st century.

Cardinal Martino, as the Holy See's Permanent Observer to the UN, addressed the First Committee of the General Assembly in 1997 as follows: 'Nuclear weapons are incompatible with the peace we seek for the 21st century. They cannot be justified. They deserve condemnation. The preservation of the Non-Proliferation Treaty demands an unequivocal commitment to their abolition'. And in 1998, also before the UN, he went even further: 'The most perilous of all the old Cold War assumptions carried into the new age is the belief that the strategy of nuclear deterrence is essential to a nation's security. Maintaining nuclear deterrence into the 21st century will not aid but impede peace. Nuclear deterrence prevents genuine nuclear disarmament. It maintains an unacceptable hegemony over non-nuclear development for the poorest half of the world's population. It is a fundamental obstacle to achieving a new age of global security.'

It seems then that far from being weapons which keep peace nuclear weapons in fact prevent peace, and we, the United Kingdom and other nations of the world who possess such weapons, are therefore also a stumbling block to peace. How can the Church remain silent, if the fundamental Easter gift of the risen Lord to his disciples is the gift of peace?

Returning to the UN, the current Permanent Observer of the Holy See, Archbishop Migliore, in May 2005, leaves us in no doubt about the clear and consistent nature of the teaching which we, the Bishops of Scotland, have a duty to pass on. 'The time has gone for finding ways to a "balance in terror"; the time has come to re-examine the whole strategy of nuclear deterrence. When the Holy See expressed its limited acceptance of nuclear deterrence during the Cold War, it was with the clearly stated condition that deterrence was only a step on the way towards progressive nuclear disarmament. The Holy See has never countenanced nuclear deterrence as a permanent measure, nor does it today when it is evident that nuclear deterrence drives the development of ever newer nuclear arms, thus preventing genuine nuclear disarmament. The Holy See again emphasises that the peace we seek in the 21st century cannot be attained by relying on nuclear weapons.'

The Pope has, within months of the start of his papacy, confirmed and strengthened this clear and consistent teaching. In January of this year he addressed a remark to those few governments such as our own who hold the world to ransom with our nuclear weapons:

> 'What can be said ... about those governments which count on nuclear arms as a means of ensuring the security of their countries? Along with countless persons of good will, one can state that this point of view is not only baneful but also completely fallacious. In a nuclear war there would be no victors, only victims. The truth of peace requires that all – whether those governments which openly or secretly possess nuclear arms, or those planning to acquire them – agree to change their course by clear and firm decisions, and strive for a progressive and concerted nuclear disarmament. The resources which would be saved could then be employed in projects of development capable of benefiting all their people, especially the poor. In this regard, one can only note with dismay the evidence of a continuing growth in military expenditure and the flourishing arms trade, while the political and juridic process established by the international community for promoting disarmament is bogged down in general indifference. How can there ever be a future of peace when investments are still made in the production of arms and in research aimed at developing new ones?' (Message for World Day of Peace, January 1st 2006)

As the Holy Father asks, how can peace have a future if we develop a replacement for Trident? With this promise of a public debate we have a golden opportunity to show that we can be a peaceful nation, not one which bullies and threatens other nations. We could, like so many other countries the world over who have dismantled their research programmes and have even given up their nuclear weapons, do this in the name of peace. Threatening behaviour changes the behaviour of the other, and peaceful action does too. This is the heart of the witness of Jesus, the heart of the Gospel, the heart of our sign of peace at Mass. We have a chance to be a nation of peace. Let us bury our belligerence, let us beat our swords into ploughshares and call on the world to follow our lead.

'I would not get too involved in the politics of independence, but I am happy that, if it is the wish of the people, Scotland becomes an independent country. ... In my travels I have had much experience of small countries and I have seen what benefits independence can bring ... Ireland would be an example of a country which has prospered since achieving independence. Additionally, other northern European countries such as Norway and Denmark exemplify the prosperity which self-determination can bring.

There is currently some frustration among the Scots about the say they have over what happens here, and that is part of what is pushing the independence movement. I can see this coming, perhaps not in the next few years, but before too long ... The recent debate on Trident is instructive. The groundswell of feeling in Scotland against the Trident missile system has highlighted a deep sense of frustration among many Scots. We have no wish to pay for or host these evil weapons, yet we have no power to remove them.'

Cardinal O'Brien quoted in Scotland on Sunday, 15 October 2006

From Suez to Iraq

Adam Price MP
Margaret Beckett MP
Jeremy Corbyn MP
Alex Salmond MP

On 31 October 2006, the House of Commons discussed the Iraq war in the first formal (albeit very brief) debate since the invasion of 2003. This debate was called by Plaid Cymru and the Scottish National Party, who had earlier initiated the campaign to impeach Tony Blair for High Crimes and Misdemeanours in relation to the invasion of Iraq (see A Case to Answer by Glen Rangwala & Dan Plesch, Spokesman £5). We excerpt some of the key speeches. This call for an Inquiry was narrowly lost – 273 votes for and 298 against.

Mr. Speaker: We now come to the main business, and I inform the House that I have selected the amendment in the name of the Prime Minister ...

Adam Price (Carmarthen, East and Dinefwr) (Plaid Cymru – the Party of Wales): I beg to move,

That this House believes that there should be a select committee of seven honourable Members, being members of Her Majesty's Privy Council, to review the way in which the responsibilities of Government were discharged in relation to Iraq and all matters relevant thereto, in the period leading up to military action in that country in March 2003 and in its aftermath.

It is an honour to move this motion on behalf of my hon. Friends and of right hon. and hon. Members on all sides of the House of Commons. It is the culmination of a long campaign, and it is a debate that is long overdue. The motion has cross-party support because the issue at its heart is far bigger than one of party politics. It is about accountability. It is about the monumental catastrophe of the Iraq war, which is the worst foreign policy disaster certainly since Suez, and possibly since Munich. It is about the morass in which, regrettably, we still find ourselves. It is also about a breakdown in our system of government – a fault line in our constitution that only we, as Parliament, can fix. Fix it we must, if there are not to be further mistakes and other Iraqs under other Prime Ministers, in which case we shall only have ourselves to blame ...

The debate on 18 March 2003 was one of the most momentous – some would say calamitous – debates in the House of Commons in modern times. The Prime Minister gave one of the great performances of his life; it was full of certainty and undaunted by doubt. But unfortunately, we now know that much of what he told us that night was false. It is no wonder that democratic politics has haemorrhaged public confidence. Only we in this Parliament can stem that flow; we can rebuild some of that trust by holding a proper inquiry into what went on.

What could an inquiry usefully do? There will inevitably be a range of views within the House, which is why we need a sufficiently broad remit. But three central questions need to be answered. How could the Government take us to war on claims that turned out to be false? When precisely was the decision to have this war made? Why has the planning for, and conduct of, the occupation proved to be so disastrous? Maybe the hon. Member for West Bromwich, West (Mr. Bailey) can give us some answers?

Mr. Adrian Bailey (West Bromwich West) (Labour/Co-op): I quite understand that the hon. Gentleman feels very deeply about this issue. But do his electorate in Wales and the electorate in Scotland consider it to be the most pressing issue affecting them?

Adam Price: I have to tell the hon. Gentleman that, like many other Members, I have constituents who are now on their third deployment to Iraq, and, yes, they want us to debate this issue. Some would argue – like the hon. Gentleman, no doubt – that we should not even have this debate while troops remain on the ground in Iraq. If we follow the logic of the Government's argument, the graver the mistake – and, therefore, the greater the danger to which our troops are exposed – the less the Government should be required to defend their record.

Mr. Douglas Hogg (Sleaford and North Hykeham) (Conservative): Would the hon. Gentleman care to remind the House that the argument that we should not debate these matters when troops are operational is precisely the argument that was made in the Norway debate, and which, happily, was rejected by people like my father, who voted against Chamberlain and brought in Churchill?

Adam Price: The right hon. and learned Gentleman makes the point very well. We need to turn the logic of the Government on its head. We need to do so precisely for the sake of our troops. We have been led into this quagmire by way of a false rationale and without a clear strategy, and we need to debate the Government's appalling record. The troops deserve nothing less ...

Almost on a weekly basis, we see senior military figure after senior military figure making yet another devastating assessment of the Government's policy-making capacity. Lord Guthrie said that the policies are cuckoo. Lord Inge said that there was a lack of clear strategy at the Ministry of Defence. Most damning of all was the verdict of the current head of the Army, who said that

> 'history will show that the planning for what happened after the initial ... war fighting phase was poor, probably based more on optimism than sound planning.'

Unfortunately, we have not seen that kind of honesty from any Government Minister to date. However, it is fair to say that the Foreign Secretary came perilously close when she said that history may judge the Iraq war to have been a disaster. Unfortunately, we do not have the luxury of waiting for history's verdict; we need some answers and action now.

A Government who were prepared to parade before our eyes dossier after dodgy dossier of carefully edited intelligence will not now let us read any of the intelligence on what is happening on the ground. We have had no comprehensive statement to date of Government policy. In February last year, the Prime Minister promised the Liaison Committee that General Luck's audit of coalition security strategy in Iraq would be published. For the record, I quote the Prime Minister:

> 'I have seen a draft that is still under discussion ... When there is a finished article, it will be published.'

It never was.

Before the Government come back and say, 'That was not our fault; the decision not to publish was made in Washington' – like so many other foreign policy decisions under this Government – I should point out to Treasury Ministers that they have not published a single word of Sir Ronnie Flanagan's assessment of the UK's contribution to Iraqi security sector reform, which was completed 10 months ago. Of course we understand that parts of these reports have to be withheld for security reasons, but does the Foreign Secretary really believe that Parliament can do its duty in holding the Government to account if we get no information about their strategy?

There are two Iraqs: the Iraq of George Bush and the Prime Minister, where things are going to plan and getting better all the time; and the real Iraq of murder and mayhem, whose future is uncertain. The state of denial that characterises the Government's policy now mirrors the state of delusion that characterised their policy in the run-up to war. The Prime Minister told us that night that it was 'beyond doubt' that Iraq had weapons of mass destruction, even though the intelligence supplied was packed with doubt. He rattled off the huge quantities of WMD that he said had been left unaccounted for. Then he treated us to the punch-line:

> 'We are asked now seriously to accept that in the last few years – contrary to all history, contrary to all intelligence – Saddam decided unilaterally to destroy those weapons. I say that such a claim is palpably absurd.' – [*Official Report*, 18 March 2003; Vol. 401, c. 762.]

Well, not as things turned out. In my more uncharitable moments, I am reminded of that famous Aneurin Bevan put-down during the Suez crisis. He said, 'If Sir Anthony Eden is sincere in what he is saying – and he may be, he may be – then he is too stupid to be Prime Minister.' ... Before I give way to the hon. Gentleman, I should like to state as a matter of record that I do not believe that the Prime Minister is stupid; that is a wholly unwarranted and unfounded accusation.

Dr. Nick Palmer (Broxtowe) (Labour): The difficulty that I and many others have with the idea of a fresh inquiry is the partisan response to the previous four inquiries, whereby those who did not wish to accept what they heard simply rejected them as whitewashes. Does the hon. Gentleman accept the Butler inquiry, the Hutton inquiry and the all-party inquiries that we have already had?

Adam Price: I have heard this charge of political opportunism – *[Interruption.]* Well, I have to tell the hon. Gentleman that, facing as we are elections in Wales and Scotland, and given that we have one of the most unpopular Prime Ministers in history, political opportunism should mean that we would like to keep him there. In fact, we are doing what is right on a cross-party basis. On the inquiries to which the hon. Gentleman referred, the key issue is: how can the Butler and Hutton inquiries have been genuinely independent of the Executive when their remit and membership were decided by the Prime Minister himself? When you are in the dock, Mr. Speaker, you are usually not allowed to make decisions about the charge sheet, the judge and the jury.

Richard Ottaway (Croydon, South) (Conservative): Does the hon. Gentleman recall that during the debate on the Hutton inquiry the Prime Minister actually confessed that he was unaware that there was evidence that the weapons of mass destruction for which he was looking were just defensive weapons – artillery shells or small-calibre weaponry? He was unaware of that at the time, as was Hutton, so we had a situation in which the Prime Minister was making representations to the House on evidence that he did not understand and had not read.

Adam Price: Absolutely. The responsibility of Ministers to tell the truth is not just in making sure that they say what they believe to be true, but testing it against the facts – actually getting into the detail – and there is plenty of evidence, as the hon. Gentleman says, that that did not happen in that case.

Angela Browning (Tiverton and Honiton) (Conservative): Is not this symptomatic of the way the Government addresses such important issues? They held several narrowly defined inquiries, rather as they did with foot and mouth, so that we never got the full picture, which is of course very much to their benefit.

Adam Price: Absolutely. The wording of our motion reflects the wording of the Franks inquiry, so that there can be a broad-ranging inquiry and we can learn lessons, to avoid repeating mistakes in the future …

Mark Fisher (Stoke-on-Trent, Central) (Lab) Does the hon. Gentleman share my view that one of the things at stake this afternoon is the credibility of Parliament, and that the key responsibilities of Parliament are to scrutinise the Executive and hold it to account? If we fail to fulfil those responsibilities in relation to the Iraq war we shall further deepen the growing and worrying imbalance between Parliament and the Executive.

Hon. Members: Hear, hear.

Adam Price: The hon. Member for Stoke-on-Trent, Central (Mark Fisher) has laid bare the constitutional question, which is at the heart of the debate, about restoring the balance of power between Parliament and the Executive.

Lembit Öpik (Montgomeryshire) (Liberal Democrat): Some have accused the hon. Gentleman of opportunism in choosing to debate this subject on an Opposition day, but does he agree that the people of Wales are keen to get to the truth of the matter and that what we really need today is a sober and considered debate rather than point-scoring – primarily by a very defensive Government? Does he hope that rather than putting party political interests first we can make the interests of democracy and our mistakes in Iraq the primary consideration in our debate?

Adam Price: I agree, and I pay tribute to courageous Members on both sides of the House who have declared support against their party line. Some things are genuinely more important than party politics, and it is a good day for parliamentary democracy when we see beyond party loyalty and look at issues of principle ...

I want to return to some of the Prime Minister's statements that were out of kilter with much of what he was being told. To give just one example, on 3 April 2002 he said: 'We know that he' – Saddam Hussein – 'has stockpiles of major amounts of chemical and biological weapons.'

But in the previous month, the most that the Joint Intelligence Committee could come up with was:

> 'We believe Iraq retains some production equipment, and some small stocks of chemical warfare agent precursors, and may have hidden small quantities of agents and weapons.'

So 'may' became 'we know' and 'small quantities' became 'major stockpiles'; that was the pattern in the presentation of the case. Small changes in emphasis and the selective use of intelligence were repeatedly used to transform a threat from minor to dire and doubtful to definite, and caveats and caution to blood-chilling certainties.

Evidence that would have undermined the case was held back. The Prime Minister frequently cited the defection of Hussein Kamel, Saddam Hussein's son-in-law, and his admission in 1995 that Iraq had indeed had an extensive WMD programme. However, what the Prime Minister omitted to tell the House was that Hussein Kamel also told UN inspectors in 1995 that he had personally ordered the destruction of all biological, chemical and nuclear weapons, and that that had happened.

Most indefensible of all was justification of the war in Iraq on the basis that it would reduce the likelihood of a terrorist attack, even though the intelligence services were saying the opposite at the time.

Jeremy Corbyn (Islington, North) (Labour): Does the hon. Gentleman also concede that any inquiry should look in some detail at the circumstances under which the UN weapons inspectors, led by Hans Blix, were withdrawn from Iraq in January 2003 and not allowed to go back, having confirmed that they believed with 99 per cent certainty that there were no such weapons of mass destruction in Iraq?

Adam Price: Absolutely. I entirely I agree with the hon. Gentleman ...

As we have learned over the past few days, with the leaked Cabinet minute and the leaked national intelligence estimate from the United States, the invasion of Iraq has increased the threat of terrorist attacks. It is a sad indictment of the Government that we learn more from leaked Cabinet papers than we ever do from a Cabinet Minister speaking at the Dispatch Box. I hope that this afternoon will be an honourable exception.

Another critical issue surrounded by confusion and controversy was the timing of the decision to go to war. We were told right up to the last few days before the debate in the House that no decision had been taken, but there is now compelling evidence that the Prime Minister had already made a decision to invade a year earlier. As early as March 2002, the Prime Minister's foreign policy adviser, Sir David Manning, was assuring Condoleezza Rice of the Prime Minister's unbudgeable support for regime change. Days later, Sir Christopher Meyer sent a dispatch to Downing Street detailing how he repeated that commitment to the US Deputy Defence Secretary. The ambassador added that the Prime Minister would need a cover for military action:

> 'I then went through the need to wrong-foot Saddam on the inspectors and the UN Security Council resolutions.'

Yet throughout that period, the Prime Minister was insisting that the war was not inevitable and no decision had been made.

Most incredibly of all, in the most recent leaked memorandum, we read that, in a meeting with the Prime Minister, the President even suggested provoking a war with Saddam by flying a US spy plane bearing UN colours over Iraq and enticing the Iraqis to take a shot at it. That is the clearest suggestion yet that the UN was being used not to prevent war, but as a pretext for beginning it.

Tom Levitt (High Peak) (Labour): Will the hon. Gentleman tell the House whether, in his preparation for this debate, he had discussions with any representatives of the Iraqi Government? Has he had representations from the Iraqi trade union movement? Is it not right that the voice of ordinary Iraqi people who support their democratic Government and the actions taken should be heard in this debate?

Adam Price: I would welcome the opportunity to go to Iraq. I have been trying to go. I was told by the former Foreign Secretary that it was not safe for a Member of Parliament to go to Iraq. That is a sad indictment of the state of affairs on the ground. Those who will support the motion include Members who opposed the war and those who supported it ...

There is no shame in changing one's mind when new facts come to light. Ask the Attorney-General. He changed his mind three times in three weeks. He finally decided on 13 March 2003, after talking things through with his secretary, that his 7 March opinion was wrong after all and that, to quote the Attorney-General's recent disclosure to the Information Commissioner,

'the better view was that a further resolution was not legally necessary'.

Incredibly, that U-turn was not based on a detailed paper setting out the legal arguments. The Attorney-General who, by his own admission, is not an expert in international law, did not ask for legal advice until after he had come to his decision. *[Interruption.]* The Minister is shaking his head. I am reading from the Government's own disclosure to the Information Commissioner, which states:

'It was also decided to prepare a statement setting out the Attorney's view of the legal position and to send instructions to counsel to help in the preparation of that public statement.'

So the Attorney-General decided what the legal position was, and then asked for legal advice. You could not make it up, Mr. Speaker – well, you could if you were the Attorney-General, apparently.

The Attorney-General went on in the same disclosure statement to admit, crucially, that the revival argument – the notion that the use of force authorised by resolution 678 from the first Gulf war was capable of being revived by the Security Council – 'was and remains controversial'. Finally, a full three years on from the invasion, we have an unequivocal admission from the Attorney-General that his statement to the House that the war was legal was 'controversial' – his word, not mine.

Chris Bryant (Labour): The hon. Gentleman has said one thing this afternoon with which I wholeheartedly agree: the people of Wales will be looking at the debate with interest. However, many service families will want to know his view not about the beginnings of the war and whether troops should have gone to Iraq in the first place, but about whether they should remain there now. Is it his position that they should leave immediately?

Adam Price: With the greatest respect to the hon. Gentleman, he knows my position because we debated that a week ago. We are having a different debate, but my position – *[Interruption.]* I would gladly debate this with the Prime Minister any time. Let us have … this debate now. I would welcome the opportunity to have a debate about the withdrawal – *[Interruption.]*

Mr. Speaker: Order. Mr. Hall, it is not your function to heckle an hon. Member constantly, especially when I have given an instruction. I am looking at a few other Members who should behave themselves as well.

Adam Price: There is a fundamental breakdown at the heart of the Government that is continuing to affect decisions that are being made now. The Government have made a catalogue of errors that have resulted in problems on the ground. As hon. Members have said, the problem was that we had not government by Cabinet, but government by cabal. The delicate checks and balances of our constitution were swept away. Cabinet was sidelined and Parliament was misled – [Hon. Members: 'Order!'] I did not say by whom.

Mr. Speaker: Order. The hon. Gentleman is in order.

Adam Price: There is a problem at the heart of our constitution and tonight we need to reapply the constitutional brakes. The military men have been lining up to criticise and so have the mandarins. A letter from Sir Michael Quinlan, of all people, a former permanent secretary at the Ministry of Defence, said that the Prime Minister

> 'exerted or connived ... to mould legal advice to his preference and failed to disclose fully ... even that moulded advice; and ... so arranged the working of the cabinet that colleagues had no timely or systematic opportunity to consider the merits of his policy in an informed manner'.

Lord Butler made the same point in an interview in *The Spectator.* He pointed out that decisions were made on the prime ministerial sofa, rather than in meetings with minutes around the Cabinet table, with all that that meant for both the quality of, and proper accountability for, decision making. Pluralism in the Government, a proper role for Parliament and the Cabinet and a truly independent civil service are there to act as a check on hubris in government. That is why we need to recalibrate the constitution of this United Kingdom and rebalance power for the benefit of Parliament, at the expense of an over-mighty Executive. We are otherwise reduced to the sorry spectacle of an Attorney-General changing his mind to save his political master's skin.

Let us remind ourselves once again of the central fact: we fought the war because of an arsenal of weapons that proved to be non-existent. Many thousands of people have paid with their lives for that mistake, and the same mirage of deception and disinformation continues to cloud our understanding of what is happening on the ground.

Mr. Denis MacShane (Rotherham) (Labour): To clarify the point for my understanding, will the hon. Gentleman have the courtesy to tell the House whether he thinks that British troops should withdraw now?

Adam Price: We had a full debate, which I led, and my position is absolutely clear. Where was the right hon. Gentleman?

The constant hailing of non-existent progress by the Government is an insult to those who genuinely appreciate what is really happening in a worsening situation.

' ... When Adam Price MP, the Honourable Member for Carmarthen East and Dinefwr, produced a report laying out the grounds for impeachment [of Tony Blair], few gave it credence. One exception, typically, was the then father of the House, Tam Dalyell, who said: "I think as a document it requires refutation in some detail. What they have produced is a perfectly serious document that makes a coherent case." Dalyell warned ministers of the dangers of "dismissing it as a joke", but they didn't listen.

Undeterred by his initial setback, Price changed tack and tabled a motion calling for a committee of seven senior MPs to conduct an inquiry into the events leading up to the war on Iraq and the aftermath of the conflict. It was this motion that finally led to the debate of 31 October, which Blair had spent three years trying to avoid.

That the government came within 25 votes of defeat is a tribute to Price's tenacity. Anyone watching in the chamber on that afternoon would have to agree that his sober and moving speech was that of a fine parliamentarian ...'

Martin Bright, New Statesman, 6 November 2006

It is a scandal that, as yet, not a single Minister has unequivocally admitted that things in Iraq have gone wrong. Both in the run-up to the war and in its aftermath the Government's policy has been characterised by a cocktail of wishful thinking, self-delusion and evasion. The sequence of events that led us to commit our armed forces to a war that was illegal and unnecessary is as yet unexplained. The strategy for removing them remains unpublished. The inquiry that we are calling for is not only essential to understanding what happened three and a half years ago; it is imperative in understanding where we go from here. It is impossible truly to discern the problems on the ground in Iraq unless we appreciate what went wrong – the mistakes and misjudgments that took us there in the first place.

History does not repeat itself, as Mark Twain once said, but it does rhyme. Fifty years ago today, our Government began bombing Egypt under the cover of darkness. That invasion, too, was based on a falsehood. Anthony Eden secretly colluded with Israel and France, and kept Parliament in the dark. It is a matter of debate as to whether the Prime Minister deliberately deceived us, but one way or another we were certainly misled. The evidence clearly suggests that he had privately assured President Bush that he would join the invasion. Here was a Prime Minister so deluded by his determination to do what he believed to be right that he began to think not as *primus inter pares* but as an acting head of state. It is time now to tell the Prime Minister and all future Prime Ministers that they are not presidents, and that the policy of this United Kingdom does not always have to be the policy of the United States.

The Secretary of State for Foreign and Commonwealth Affairs (Margaret Beckett): I beg to move, To leave out from 'House' to the end of the Question, and to add instead thereof:

'recognising that there have already been four separate independent committees of inquiry into military action in Iraq and recognising the importance of learning all possible lessons from military action in Iraq and its aftermath, declines at this time, whilst the whole effort of the Government and the armed forces is directed towards improving the condition of Iraq, to make a proposal for a further inquiry which would divert attention from this vital task.'

The motion before the House today calls for the creation of a new inquiry

'to review the way in which the responsibilities of Government were discharged in relation to Iraq...in the period leading up to military action in that country in March 2003 and in its aftermath.'

The question that I want to put to the House is not so much why – because of course it is perfectly sensible and legitimate to say that there will come a time when these issues will be explored in the round and in full, so that we can learn whatever lessons we can from them – but rather, why this specific inquiry, and much more to the point, why now.

Unlike at the time of the Falklands war we now have a framework of Select Committees that carry out independent inquiries. I recognise that the official Opposition have tabled an amendment that suggests a Falklands-type inquiry in the next Session of Parliament, without pointing out that that begins in just two weeks. I am afraid that I think that that, too, is not sensible. It avoids none of the dangers of sending the wrong signals at the wrong time and distracting resources and attention from where they are most needed. Indeed, it risks appearing to set a deadline for our operations in Iraq which would be politically and militarily damaging ...

There have already been two parliamentary Committee reports on Iraq: the Foreign Affairs Committee report, 'The Decision to go to War in Iraq', and the Intelligence and Security Committee report, 'Iraqi Weapons of Mass Destruction – Intelligence and Assessments'. There have been two further independent reports: the Hutton inquiry into the circumstances surrounding the death of Dr. David Kelly CMG, and the Butler review of intelligence on weapons of mass destruction. Is this the moment to take a decision and a step of the kind recommended in the motion? My answer is a resounding no. There is absolutely nothing in the unquestionably difficult and delicate situation in Iraq today that makes this the obvious and right time.

Mr. Edward Leigh (Gainsborough) (Conservative): So the Foreign Secretary can give a firm commitment to the House that an inquiry will be held as soon as our troops leave?

Margaret Beckett: What I am saying to the House, and what I shall say repeatedly, is that this is not the time for making these decisions. I will tell the hon. Gentleman why. Our words in the House today will be heard a very long way away. They can be heard by our troops, who are already in great danger in Iraq. They can be heard by the Iraqi people and by their Government, many of whose members I know many hon. Members in all parts of the House have met – people whose bravery and fortitude is humbling and who still need our support, not the rehashing of issues that have been gone over umpteen times in the House.

Mark Pritchard (The Wrekin) (Conservative): The Foreign Secretary asks why now. What if, God forbid, Parliament has to vote to send our brave armed servicemen and women into war again? We need an inquiry now to ensure that the British people can once again trust the Government. I do not think that that is possible, but I hope that in the House today the Foreign Secretary will agree to an inquiry in order that future wars can be built on trust and on the full backing of Parliament and the people, without mass deception.

Margaret Beckett: I do not take any lectures from Conservative Members, who never, ever gave the House a vote about sending troops into action, including on some occasions when I do not necessarily dispute that it was right to send them, including on occasions without United Nations authority.

Mr. John Maples (Stratford-on-Avon) (Consvative): The Foreign Secretary prayed in aid the [Foreign Affairs] Select Committee's report. I was a member of that Committee, and I have to say to her that her predecessor and the Government obstructed the Committee's proceedings at every stage possible, refusing to produce witnesses and documents.

Margaret Beckett: I am sorry; I do not accept that in the slightest, and I shall tell the hon. Gentleman why. I followed – from a slight distance, I concede – many of the discussions and many of the requests from the Select Committee ... I followed those matters as carefully as I could, and I observed – and I observed it from Committee members who had ministerial experience – people asking for papers and for disclosures which they, as former Ministers and experienced Members of the House, would never for a single second have contemplated disclosing. I reject utterly the suggestion that the Committee did not get full support.

Mr. Frank Field (Birkenhead) (Lab): Does the Foreign Secretary think I am exceptional, in the sense that not one of my constituents has asked me to press for an inquiry into the causes of the war? However, many of my constituents are troubled about which moves we should make in the best interests of the people of Iraq. Many of them would be appalled at the fact that much of the debate is looking backwards. There will come a time when accounts are settled, but my constituents are desperately concerned about the right moves for the future.

Margaret Beckett: I am grateful to my right hon. Friend, who I know is held in high regard in all parts of the House. What he says is also my experience, and I expect that he speaks for Members in all parts of the House who may not all wish to acknowledge it ...

What happens in the House today will be heard not only by those in Iraq – the people and the Government – but by those whose intention it is to do us harm, whether in Iraq or beyond. Again, I ask the House to consider whether now is the time to send a signal – every Member of the House knows in their heart that this is true – which many will undoubtedly interpret as a weakening of our commitment ...

There is an important tradition in the House that all political parties give our troops and are seen to give our troops their full support while they are in conflict. That is a precedent which it would be dangerous to break.

Mr. Kenneth Clarke (Rushcliffe) (Con): The Foreign Secretary would get rid of the dissention this afternoon and send out a fairly united message if she said that there will be a Franks-type inquiry into the invasion of Iraq and its aftermath as soon as the troops are withdrawn. I cannot understand whether she is saying that she accepts the need for such an inquiry but that the time is not ripe, or whether she is saying in weasel words that we have had enough inquiries already. If she accepted what will be forced on the Government in any event – a Franks-type inquiry when the hostilities have ceased – we would send a united message from this House.

Margaret Beckett: I am surprised that the right hon. and learned Gentleman cannot understand what I am saying, because it is clear and simple: today is not the time for making these decisions. *[Interruption.]* ... As for the right hon. and learned Gentleman's contention that a Franks-type inquiry is required, I refer him to the discussion in this House in July 2003 when one of my former colleagues, Mr. Tam Dalyell, who was summoned to give evidence to the Franks inquiry, commented on how inadequate it was ...

It is now more than three years since the Government committed UK forces, as part of an international coalition led by the United States, to military action against Saddam Hussein's regime in Iraq. Saddam Hussein had repeatedly and openly defied the authority of the United Nations, and before UN Security Council resolution 1441, which was carried unanimously because of the unanimous conviction that he represented a serious danger to the international community, he already stood in material breach of 17 separate UN resolutions. He refused fully to co-operate with the weapons inspection regime imposed on him as someone who had both possessed and used weapons of mass destruction. The international community as a whole – not just the United States and the UK – believed that he had developed and wished further to develop WMD capability.

Sir Malcolm Rifkind (Kensington and Chelsea) (Conservative): Does the Foreign Secretary realise that her opposition to an inquiry into the origins of the Government's policy on Iraq would be more convincing if the Government were not simultaneously bitterly opposing any debate on the future of their policy in Iraq? Is she not ashamed that, in the three years since the war, the Government have not initiated a single debate on the subject in this Chamber? The United

States Congress was permitted a full debate on the matter as recently as June. Is it not appalling that, when the Government have been responsible for such an arrant misuse of their powers, this Chamber has not been allowed to debate the matter?

Margaret Beckett: The right hon. and learned Gentleman is talking complete nonsense, as he must be well aware. He is a former Secretary of State for Defence, and he knows that there are five defence debates a year and that there are debates on foreign policy, all of which are in Government time. Of course it is open to people to debate those issues.

Mr. Paul Keetch (Hereford) (Liberal Democrat): The Foreign Secretary seems to be saying that an inquiry now would be wrong, because our forces are in the field. Indeed, she has accused the Conservative party of never having succumbed to such a debate in the past. How does she answer the historical fact that in May 1940, while British troops were fighting and losing a campaign in Norway, a Conservative Government allowed a debate in this Chamber in which the Labour party, the Liberal party and some notable people from the Conservative party conspired to vote against the Government of the day, which led to the resignation of the then Prime Minister and the installation of a coalition Government? When our troops are in a campaign, that is surely when this House – a democracy – should be allowed to debate their conduct.

Margaret Beckett: I did not say the words that the hon. Gentleman has put into my mouth, and I am sorry if he misheard me. I continue to take the view that this is not the time for this debate. Moreover, I have been reminded that the motion to which the hon. Gentleman has referred was taken on the Adjournment and was not a motion to bind the Government of the day ...

The decision to take part in military action was not taken lightly or trivially. In an unprecedented step, it was the subject of a full debate and a vote in this House, which was right. Committing British troops to a war is one of the most solemn decisions that any Government can ever take, but we did so because we judged, and because this House judged – the hon. Member for Carmarthen, East and Dinefwr (Adam Price) talked about voices being heard; some 52 Members of this House spoke in that debate – that the threat to international peace and security was very real and very grave. The original decision to take military action provoked fierce debate in this Chamber and across the country, and I have no doubt that it will continue for much time to come; but the decisions we take in the weeks and months to come should surely have as their priority what is best for Iraq and its people, here and now, as well as the impact that any decision we make may have on our troops in the field.

Last December, more than 75 per cent of the Iraqi people elected a new Parliament under a permanent, new constitution; and let us not forget that they did so under threat of death from those who sought only destruction in Iraq. This spring, that Parliament elected a new Government of national unity representing all Iraq's main political parties, and for the first time in their history the people of Iraq began a bold attempt to share power equitably among the nation's ethnic and confessional populations ...

I do not in any way underestimate the terrible difficulties that many people in Iraq are facing. Many of them have to cope today and every day with the kind of terrorist horror which so profoundly shocked our own country last July. As I have said, their bravery in the face of that threat is humbling. The Iraqi Government, headed by Prime Minister Maliki, are barely five months into their term. From the outset, they have faced a daunting array of political and economic challenges of a kind with which any Government in the world would struggle to deal. Overshadowing all else has been a relentless and rising tide of murderous violence, some of it a very deliberate effort to destroy the fragile foundations of Iraq's democratic system.

John Baron (Billericay) (Conservative): Cannot the Foreign Secretary understand that a good part of the deep frustration expressed by this House arises because the Prime Minister refuses to come to this House and lead a debate on current and future policy on Iraq? Given General Sir Richard Dannatt's recent comments, and the fact that the situation seems to be deteriorating, will the Foreign Secretary now encourage the Prime Minister to come to this House and lead a debate?

Margaret Beckett: I am sorry, but I do not think that that is what is inspiring the comments and the mood in the House today. Perhaps it would be better if it were, but I do not believe that it is ...

Elsewhere, we have seen a spiral of retaliatory sectarian killings. Here, too, existing ethnic tensions have been carefully exploited by those who have no interest in Iraq becoming a fully functioning state and every interest in dragging it back into chaos and lawlessness. It is this violence that has held up and disrupted the supply of essential services to Iraqis; it is this violence that has meant that the political framework is taking longer to develop; and it is this violence that is holding millions of ordinary Iraqis back from a better future for themselves and their families. That is why Prime Minister Maliki has made tackling the violence his Government's highest priority. We are in Iraq at the express request of that Government and with the full support of the United Nations, and so our responsibility is to support the sovereign Government of Iraq in their objectives.

The Iraqi Government and the coalition forces are currently engaged in a critical attempt to make Baghdad more secure. In Basra, British troops are in the middle of a similarly vital mission to take on the violent extremists and lay the foundations of long-term security. The challenge faced by the Iraqi people in those two cities, as elsewhere in the country, is not purely military. Much of the current violence has political roots and it will be through determined political efforts – led by Iraqis – that it will ultimately be addressed. There can be no substitute for strong political leadership in Iraq. We have strongly supported Prime Minister

Maliki's commitment to national reconciliation and have worked hard to bring all Iraq's political and clerical leaders fully and wholeheartedly behind it, because that offers the best chance of building a consensus among Iraq's divided communities, all of whom are suffering from the current levels of violence, and of isolating those who are trying to drive the Iraqi people further from one another.

At the same time, we are urging Iraq's political leaders to move ahead without delay in taking crucial decisions on the country's future. We are offering strong support for their work to reach agreement by the end of the year on a new law setting out the future of the oil and gas sector, which is central to Iraq's economic regeneration. We are actively encouraging the Iraqi Parliament to pass new legislation – again, by the end of the year – setting out how the militias can be disbanded and reintegrated into society. We are pushing the Iraqi Parliament for a decision on reforms to the process of de-Ba'athification, as well as on how the agreement to review the new constitution will be implemented. Those are all difficult as well as complex issues – otherwise, they would have been solved long ago – but if we get them right, we can create a new, more positive political dynamic in the country.

Prime Minister Maliki wants to make rapid progress towards the Iraqi Government and security forces assuming responsibility for the country's security.

Bob Russell (Colchester) (LD): While praising our troops' contribution both in the war and today, will the Foreign Secretary please return to and address the motion?

Margaret Beckett: I am explaining why the motion is so profoundly misconceived. The future of Iraq and its people is at stake, and that is what really matters. If the signal sent from the House casts doubt on our support for what is happening in Iraq, for the actions of our coalition forces, and for those who are not in our forces but who are engaged in trying to support the people of Iraq, ultimately, that will be utterly to their disadvantage ...

The Government share the Prime Minister's determination – as, I have no doubt, does every Member of the House – to see responsibility pass to Iraqi police and security forces. That is fundamental to the coalition's strategy for progressively scaling down military support to the Iraqi Government. British soldiers are doing an astounding job in the most difficult of circumstances, as they do whenever and wherever they are called on; so, too, are a large number of British civilians – civil servants, policemen and women, aid workers and many more, many of whom I met in Basra not long ago. I am sure that all Members, whatever their view of the motion, would recognise the bravery and sacrifice of those people. That contribution is essential in support of the future in Iraq.

The new Iraqi army is getting more capable and more confident. It is increasingly non-sectarian. Two of the 10 divisions of that new army have already been transferred to the direct control of the Iraqi Government, and more will follow in the coming months. Therefore, in spite of the violence, we are seeing major strides towards equipping the Iraqi Government with the tools that they need to protect their people without relying on indefinite help from the international community ...

Two entire provinces, al-Muthanna and Dhi Qar, have already been handed over to Iraqi control, and more will soon follow. In our area of responsibility in the south, we hope that Maysan province will also have been handed over by the end of the year. A central aim of our current efforts in Basra is to get that province to the point where it, too, is ready to be handed over to Iraqi lead security control. We hope that that can be accomplished at some point next spring. We share the hope recently expressed by the commander of the multinational force in Iraq that all 18 provinces can be handed over to Iraqi control by the end of 2007.

Mr. Andrew Tyrie (Chichester) (Con): This debate is not about the conduct of policy in Iraq now, but about whether we should hold a Select Committee inquiry into the way in which the war has been and will be conducted in future. My hon. Friend the Member for Stratford-on-Avon (Mr. Maples) made the valid point that the inquiry by the Foreign Affairs Committee was thwarted by the Government, which the Foreign Secretary refuted. I would like to quote what the report says –

Madam Deputy Speaker: Order. The hon. Gentleman is a very experienced Member of the House and knows that interventions must be brief.

Margaret Beckett: On the hon. Gentleman's final point, the inquiry was followed by the Intelligence and Security Committee and the Butler reports, which considered the issues in depth. I would say to him, and to those Opposition Members who have been muttering and grumbling, that what I am talking about – the present position in Iraq – is exactly the point. That position is difficult; we do not dispute that at all. It is also extremely delicate. We are at what could be a turning point in Iraq, and this is not the time to do what the hon. Member for Carmarthen, East and Dinefwr did in moving the motion, and rehash all the debates and arguments that have been held over and over again, not only in the House, but in a succession of inquiries ...

We expect the Iraqi Government to request an extension of the UN mandate under which we are currently operating until 2007, and if they ask for ongoing support, we will provide it. I take very seriously, and hold strongly, the view that at this critical juncture, when Iraq's future hangs so clearly in the balance, it would be plainly and simply wrong to heed those who argue for us just to wash our hands of responsibility and walk away.

We have been working hard in recent months with the Iraqi Government and our international partners to develop an international compact for Iraq, modelled on the Afghan compact, so that the international community can provide further involvement and support for the people of Iraq, and we are keen to use that opportunity to encourage its neighbours to engage fully in the country's stabilisation and reconstruction. An important step forward on that initiative was taken at the UN-hosted meeting that I attended in New York on 18 September, and a further preparatory meeting is taking place in Kuwait today, so critical decisions about the future of Iraq are being taken today even as we debate the issue in the House.

We would, of course, like two of Iraq's neighbours – Iran and Syria – to play a similarly positive role in promoting stability and development, although the Iraqi Government themselves are convinced that at present those two countries are doing precisely the opposite. We will continue to pressure them to take a different approach, but it would be naïve to imagine that that is a straightforward task. I have set out the objectives and strategy that we, our allies and the Iraqis are currently pursuing, and I can see no credible alternative ...

I have said, and we have repeatedly said, that neither our forces nor our civilian support staff will stay in Iraq a day longer than they are needed. For now, however, we are needed, so we stay ...

Some have argued that we should abandon the idea of preserving Iraq's territorial integrity and accept the break-up of the country. I do not believe that it would be in anyone's interest – not the Iraqi people's, not the region's, not our own – to try to partition Iraq's communities. There are no neat divisions in Iraq. Its great cities host a medley of communities. Splitting Iraq's people apart and forcing people to move from their homes would risk bloodshed on a scale far worse even than we see today, but engaging in that argument at all seems to me to miss the crucial point.

Our task in the House and in the country is not to speculate on or to predict what decisions a future Iraqi Government might or might not take. It is to unite now in support of the national Government of Iraq, who were elected by the Iraqi people to govern that country. I believe that those who tabled this motion and those who are considering supporting it have fallen into the same trap of ignoring the imperative of the present difficult situation in Iraq.

I have no doubt that there will come a time when we will want to look at the lessons learned from our full experience in Iraq, just as we have from every other major conflict in the past, but now, I repeat, is not that time. The challenges Iraq faces are, as I have set out today, acute. They will require our undivided attention and focus. Our responsibility to the people of Iraq demands nothing less.

I recognise that Conservative Members have proposed an amendment that suggests a Falklands-type inquiry in the next Session of Parliament. As I have explained, I believe that that is also unwise. Whatever anyone's view of the decisions that were made in 2003 and subsequently, it would be the wrong decision today to divert the time and energy of all those working hard to secure a better future for Iraq. I have to say that I deplore the apparent complete disinterest in the future of Iraq that some Opposition Members have displayed – *[Interruption.]* It would be a waste to divert our energies to a further inquiry ... I hope that all Members will think very carefully indeed before casting their votes tonight. It is all very well to say, as some Opposition Members have said, that it is all right to vote for the motion because they do not really support it. I fear that the parliamentary nuances will be lost on the Government of Iraq, let alone the wider international community. Furthermore, Conservative Members should reflect on with whom they will be going into the Lobby if they support the motion. Many of those who support the motion have always opposed this action. Before hon. Members decide how to vote tonight, I ask them to weigh very carefully indeed what signals will be sent out.

*　*　*

The debate continued for several hours. Jeremy Corbyn made a late contribution before Alex Salmond wound up in support of the motion before the House.

Jeremy Corbyn (Islington, North) (Lab): ...The debate is essential, and I pay tribute to the hon. Member for Carmarthen, East and Dinefwr (Adam Price) for securing it in the first place. It is a debate about our role as Members of Parliament in holding the Government and the Executive to account. That is what we are sent here for. That is why people vote in parliamentary elections. If we want to do something to restore people's confidence in the democratic process in this country, we should support the motion at 7 o'clock.

We should do that for several reasons. The inquiries that are necessary into the war in Iraq might spare us involvement in future conflicts. They will open up the books and the record on what happened in the run-up to the war in 2003. In an earlier intervention, I asked the hon. Member for Carmarthen, East and Dinefwr about just one example of that. In 2002, the Prime Minister met the President of the United States on several occasions, many summit meetings were held, troops were deployed to the theatre of war, and there were constant reports about the weapons inspectors, who were apparently having success both in ridding Iraq of any weapons of mass destruction or the ability to make them, and in reducing the appalling human rights abuses that Saddam Hussein and his regime had been committing against the people of that country. A serious process was going on.

Using our power in the Security Council, however, we prevented the weapons inspectors from going back into Iraq in January 2003. At the same time, massive public demonstrations took place, including the million-plus march in London and equivalent sized demonstrations in the USA. I had the privilege of attending the one in London, and of attending an enormous one in San Francisco. There was always huge opposition to the war in the USA, and as President Bush is about to find out next week, that opposition has grown a lot bigger. We need answers to that question about the weapons inspectors.

We also need answers to the question of the legality of the war. Let us consider the way in which United Nations Security Council resolution 1441 was constantly prayed in aid by Ministers as a justification for the war. There is no justification for war when no ever-ready, real or present threat existed, when there were no weapons of mass destruction, and when no weapons were going to be fired off at 45 minutes' notice. What we had was a President backed into a corner and troops in theatre, so we had to go for it. The war duly took place.

As other Members have pointed out, since the troops arrived in Iraq, according to *The Lancet*, 650,000 Iraqis, more than 2,000 American soldiers and more than a hundred British soldiers have lost their lives. In my involvement with the Stop the War campaign, I have met many of the families of British soldiers who lost their lives in Iraq. In my constituency, I have also met many Iraqis seeking asylum from both Saddam Hussein and the current situation. None of them praised Saddam Hussein, but all thought that the situation was now more dangerous and worse than when the invasion took place. Those views need to be heard, and the inquiries need to be held ...

I want the motion to be carried so that we establish a committee of inquiry into all the circumstances surrounding the run-up to the war, the aftermath of the war in Iraq and what we do in future. We live in a world where terrorism has been encouraged by the invasion of Iraq, and, I believe, by the continued presence in Afghanistan. If we want to live in a world of perpetual wars throughout this century, we are going the right way about it. If we want to live in a world of peace and justice, we need to examine how we got into this perilous situation, why we are continuing in it, and what we are doing to address the grievances in the world – Palestinian grievances, the gap between rich and poor, and all the other problems facing the planet. That is the way forward. We should examine our consciences and what we have done, and learn the lessons from that.

Mr. Alex Salmond (Banff and Buchan) (Scottish National Party): It is an enormous pleasure to follow the hon. Member for Islington, North (Jeremy Corbyn), because if I remember correctly he was one of 23 hon. Members who, two years ago, started the campaign to bring parliamentary accountability to the situation. Over those two years, the motion put forward for discussion has changed – it has had to – and tonight 170 Members from both sides of the Chamber, including Labour, Liberal Democrat, Scottish National Party, Plaid Cymru, Independent and Conservative Members, are brought together to endorse the motion before the House.

Mr. Jim Devine (Livingston) (Labour): Will the hon. Gentleman give way?

Mr. Salmond: I hope that the hon. Gentleman will give me a minute or two to develop my point first. I certainly will not forget him: he signed the early-day motion. I just hope that he has the courage to follow his conscience into the Lobby this evening. No doubt he will tell us in a minute or two.

I pay tribute to the SNP, Plaid Cymru and the Liberal Democrat party for their position on the war. It was not so difficult for us to follow through on that position because we are united as parties, but when Labour and Conservative Members differ from their party it may take a great deal of moral courage to go against what their Front-Bench spokesmen say. The fact that the motion is being debated in the House is a demonstration of Back-Bench responsibility. It is the duty of Parliament to hold the Government to account.

Last Wednesday, I remember that the Prime Minister told the hon. Member for Billericay (Mr. Baron) that he would be delighted to debate Iraq in the House 'at any time.' Clearly, tonight was not convenient for the Prime Minister. He would have been well advised to turn up, because the Foreign Secretary did not give him the sort of defence that I would like her to give me, if my conduct was being examined ...

Mr. Devine: I am grateful to the hon. Gentleman for giving way. Let me say to him, in a comradely way, 'You tube', because I have just been watching him on YouTube, where he says:

'On Halloween the ghost of Iraq will return to haunt Blair. The SNP and Plaid Cymru have put down a motion to impeach Blair and hold him to account.'

What is it to be – impeachment or an inquiry?

Mr. Salmond: The hon. Gentleman should accept that we ought not to allow the Leader of the Opposition to be the only politician on YouTube. I would not want to condemn the youngsters of this country to such a situation. If the hon. Gentleman had been listening, rather than preparing his question, he would know that I referred to precisely that issue – to the 23 Members, including the hon. Member for Islington, North, who came together to introduce a motion of impeachment. However, it was argued that we should change the motion for two reasons. The first was to broaden the base, because it is not just the Prime Minister who is responsible. Ministers have collective responsibility, and it was Government policy that took us into Iraq. The second reason, as the hon. Gentleman probably knows even though he is relatively new, was that the process of impeachment is a trial in Parliament by the House of Lords. Given what I found out recently about the complexion of Members in the House of Lords, I now think that Members of the House of Commons are the right people to hold such an inquiry. I hope that that satisfies the hon. Gentleman.

I am glad to see that the Foreign Secretary has returned to her place. Earlier, she made the extraordinary proposition that it was not the right time to hold an inquiry. Apparently, we can allow an inquiry by Lord Butler and Lord Hutton when our troops are in the field, but not a parliamentary inquiry. What kind of argument is that? I know that the Foreign Secretary only recently took up her post, and perhaps she is not yet fully in command of her brief, but when she was asked a direct question by the hon. Member for Stratford-on-Avon (Mr. Maples) – a member of the Foreign Affairs Committee – about its inquiry, she said that there had been no Government obstruction of that inquiry. That is remarkable, because I have before me the title of the first special report of the Foreign Affairs Committee, which reads 'Implications for the Work of the House and its Committees of the Government's Lack of Co-operation with the Foreign Affairs Committee's Inquiry into the Decision to Go to War in Iraq'. If the Foreign Secretary wants to be a success in her position and to defend the Prime Minister, she should familiarise herself with the work of that Select Committee.

I was interested to hear the Foreign Secretary pray in aid my old friend Tam Dalyell against the Franks committee. I am in no doubt whatever about which Lobby Tam Dalyell would go into this evening, if he were still in the House. There are three basic arguments for the motion. The first concerns parliamentary accountability. It is pretty unprecedented in recent times, but the hon. Member for Louth and Horncastle (Sir Peter Tapsell) reminded me that Lord Liverpool, in 1855, fell on just such a motion –

Sir Peter Tapsell: Lord Aberdeen.

Mr. Salmond: Yes, it was Lord Aberdeen who, in 1855, fell on just such a motion, but I do not think that the hon. Gentleman is claiming to have personal knowledge of that debate. Nonetheless, we should be reminded by history that it is not unprecedented for a motion to have such results. I have listened to every word of this debate, unlike the Foreign Secretary, and so can say that we should have such debates more often in the House, because they do us enormous credit. The debate is on current events in Iraq, as well as the history of the war. That is why the motion refers to the war 'and its aftermath'.

Jim Sheridan (Paisley and Renfrewshire, North) (Lab): Will the hon. Gentleman give way?

Mr. Salmond: I will, in a second or two.

The Foreign Secretary shook her head when my hon. Friend the Member for Carmarthen, East and Dinefwr (Adam Price), who moved the motion, suggested that she had admitted that historians might judge the Iraqi adventure a foreign policy disaster. I have with me the transcript of her interview on BBC Radio 4. Asked whether historians might ultimately conclude that the war was a 'foreign policy disaster' for Britain, the Foreign Secretary replied:

> 'Yes, they may. Then again, they may not.'

Margaret Beckett: I am reluctant to intervene, but what the hon. Member for Carmarthen, East and Dinefwr (Adam Price) actually claimed was that I had said that the war was a disaster. I did not say that; I would never say that, and I am sick and tired of journalists putting words into my mouth, as they so frequently do.

Mr. Salmond: Asked whether historians would judge Iraq to have been a 'foreign policy disaster', the Foreign Secretary said:

> 'Yes, they may. Then again, they may not.'

She will forgive us if that does not fill the House with confidence about her confidence in the policy on Iraq. She should accept that Members may judge, before historians do, whether the policy has been a disaster. Members might sometimes offer the Government some wisdom that could change the situation and – who knows? – alter the course of events and save lives … the third reason for supporting the motion concerns what happens if the same circumstances arise in future. Surely we should look to the future. What happens if there is another conflict that the House is misled into supporting, and if we are bounced into another Iraq? The back-stop of full, parliamentary accountability will make any Government, and any Prime Minister, think again before taking the course that the Prime Minister took.

Clare Short: Does the hon. Gentleman agree that we do not have an exit strategy on Iraq, and that the chaos can continue for many years to come? Does he agree that if we are to decide on an exit strategy, we first need to know why we were there, and does he agree that we should not accede to the American aspiration to set up permanent bases, which will almost certainly mean a permanent insurgency?

Mr. Salmond: I agree with the right hon. Lady. I understand that she was at the Cabinet table when the decisions were being made, and I respect her opinion. Her doubts carry a great deal of credibility – perhaps more credibility than the words of the former Home Secretary, the right hon. Member for Sheffield, Brightside (Mr. Blunkett). He accused my hon. Friend the Member for Carmarthen, East and Dinefwr of impugning the motives of the Attorney-General. I read the former Home Secretary's memoirs only a few days ago, and, as I understand it, they suggest that the Chancellor of the Exchequer may have fallen in behind the Prime Minister only because he was frightened of losing his job. When it comes to impugning motives, my hon. Friend can take lessons from the former Home Secretary.

Jim Sheridan: Those of us who know the hon. Gentleman from his work in Scotland know that he is a straight-talking guy, so before Members from both sides of the House go into the Lobby, can he tell us, unequivocally, whether he has said today that the motion is about the impeachment of the prime Minister? Can he answer that question?

Mr. Salmond: The motion began as an impeachment motion. [Hon. Members: 'Answer!'] We tabled the motion that appears on the Order Paper to secure maximum unity across the House. It is concerned with parliamentary responsibility and accountability. I suggest that the hon. Gentleman read it and follow his conscience by joining us in the Lobby.
    Many of us remember the debate on Iraq in which the Prime Minister said that it was 'palpably absurd' not to believe that there were weapons of mass destruction in Iraq. He told us that he had never made the argument for regime change when defending the decision to invade Iraq. He has made that argument many times since the invasion, because clearly he can no longer make the argument about weapons of mass destruction. Those are not matters of opinion, but of fact – we know that there were not any weapons of mass destruction in Iraq,

and that the American justification that al-Qaeda was involved was tenuous at best. There was no connection with 9/11 to justify the invasion and the casualty toll as a result of the action is a matter of fact: 120 British soldiers and 2,821 American soldiers are dead. Tens of thousands – perhaps hundreds of thousands – of Iraqi civilians are dead. Those are the consequences of the decision by the House.

Suez was raised a number of times in our debate, but casualties there did not approach the total that I have just given the House. Certainly, lives were lost, but not to the extent that they have been lost in Iraq – 16 British soldiers were lost at Suez, every one a tragedy; 1,650 Egyptians were killed, every one a tragedy. Compared with the consequences that have befallen us in Iraq, however, Suez is as nothing. Yesterday, the Prime Minister and the Chancellor of the Exchequer announced a campaign to save the world from climate change. They have spent $5 billion in Iraq and the Americans have spent $200 billion. What if those resources had been devoted to saving the planet, rather than starting an illegal war?

Finally, our genuinely cross-party motion provides a chance to achieve parliamentary accountability. It is an opportunity for the House of Commons to live up to our constituents' expectations. It has been said that our soldiers would be discouraged if the motion were agreed, but they would be discouraged only if they thought that the House had forgotten them and was frightened to debate the implications of Iraq. They would be discouraged if they thought that Members were not prepared to table motions or consider how we can get out of the morass into which we have been led.

It is the Government who refuse to debate or introduce policies, but it is the House of Commons, by voting in the Division Lobbies tonight, that can finally hold them to account.

'Why is it the Scottish National Party that is making the running on so many issues in Westminster right now? What are the other 644 members of Parliament doing? I think we should be told.

It was the SNP MP Angus Brendan MacNeil who made the original complaint to the Metropolitan Police over those secret loans from subsequently ennobled businessmen. That action has provoked a crisis within No. 10, and brought to light a corrupt system which has not only made Lords reform inevitable, but has also raised serious questions about the integrity of the Prime Minister.

It was an SNP motion calling for an inquiry into Iraq which brought the government within 25 votes of defeat in the Commons. That was an inspired move ...

The SNP have tabled another ingenious motion, this time to the Queen's Speech. The amendment calls on the government to deliver a statement and a vote on an exit strategy from Iraq   Kenneth Clarke, the former Chancellor, has no problems in supporting the SNP motion on the Queen's Speech. So why haven't opposition MPs been engaging in creative proceduralism ...?'

Iain Macwhirter, The Guardian, 14 November 2006

THE BERTRAND RUSSELL PEACE FOUNDATION

DOSSIER

2007   Number 22

COUNTING THE IRAQI DEAD

In 2004, The Lancet published an authoritative survey of mortality in Iraq (see Spokesman 84), which generated great controversy. The Lancet has now published follow-up work by three authors of the original survey, Professors Gilbert Burnham and Riyadh Lafta and Doctor Les Roberts, together with Dr. Shannon Doocy. In this short excerpt, they discuss their latest findings, which have not been credibly challenged.

'We estimate that, as a consequence of the coalition invasion of March 18, 2003, about 655,000 Iraqis have died above the number that would be expected in a non-conflict situation, which is equivalent to about 2·5% of the population in the study area. About 601,000 of these excess deaths were due to violent causes. Our estimate of the post-invasion crude mortality rate represents a doubling of the baseline mortality rate, which, by the Sphere standards, constitutes a humanitarian emergency.

Our estimate of the pre-invasion crude or all-cause mortality rate is in close agreement with other sources. The post-invasion crude mortality rate increased significantly from pre-invasion figures, and showed a rising trend. The increasing number of violent deaths follows trends of bodies counted by mortuaries, as well as those reported in the media and by the Iraq Body Count.

Application of the mortality rates reported here to the period of the 2004 survey gives an estimate of 112,000 (69,000–155,000) excess deaths in Iraq in that period. Thus, the data presented here validates our 2004 study, which conservatively estimated an excess mortality of nearly 100,000 as of September, 2004.'

CENTRAL ASIA: A NUCLEAR-WEAPONS-FREE ZONE

The foreign ministers of the five Central Asian States — Kazakhstan, Kyrgyzstan, Tajikistan, Turkmenistan, and Uzbekistan — signed a treaty establishing a Central Asian Nuclear Weapon Free Zone (CANWFZ) on 8 September 2006. The signing of the treaty went forward despite objections by the United States, the United Kingdom and France. The new zone joins four others covering Latin America and the Caribbean, the South Pacific, South-east Asia, and Africa. Some of these Central

Asian states previously had nuclear weapons on their territory as well as sites for nuclear tests. Nuclear-armed powers in the region include Russia, China, Pakistan, and Indian. At the signing ceremony, Kazakh Foreign Minister Kasymoshomart Tokayev underlined the symbolic significance of the new zone, stating: 'The countries of our region declared a firm commitment to the principles of disarmament and non-proliferation. This is our contribution to ensuring global security.'

CLUSTER BOMBS IN KOSOVO

The British Government has argued at the European Court of Human Rights that it should not be held accountable for human rights breaches by British troops in the course of military operations abroad. The Grand Chamber of 17 Strasbourg judges has to decide whether the European Convention on Human Rights applies to the military operations of European troops abroad.

Britain and five other European countries have intervened in a case brought against France for failing to safeguard the lives of two Kosovan boys by ensuring that cluster bombs dropped by Nato forces were cleared up. One boy was killed and his brother was blinded and disfigured. The seven governments argue that no international operations of this kind could ever be mounted in the future if the participating states were told that they would be held accountable before the European Court for any violations of human rights they committed in the course of their military operations.

The Strasbourg case is being brought on behalf of Gadaf Behrami and his brother, Bekir, who were playing with other boys in the hills in the Sipolje area of Mitrovica, Kosovo, in March 2000, when they came across a number of undetonated cluster bombs left behind after the Nato bombardment in 1999. The Behrami family had been in Switzerland for nine years as refugees and had returned to Kosovo only the year before, thinking their homeland was now safe.

One of the boys threw a cluster bomb into the air. It detonated and killed 11-year-old Gadaf and seriously injured Bekir, then aged nine. At the time Mitrovica was within the sector of Kosovo for which a multinational brigade led by France was responsible. It was one of four brigades making up the international security force (Kfor) presence in Kosovo, mandated by a UN security council resolution.

Lawyers for the Behrami family say that despite the French Kfor troops' express mandate to ensure a safe and secure environment for returning refugees, they failed to take any steps to remove the Nato cluster bombs which they knew were in a particular location in the hills near Mitrovica. Although they were aware of the risk to local children, they took no steps to inform the local families of the dangers, fence off or mark the area, or dispose of the unexploded ordnance.

Unmik, the UN operation administering Kosovo, introduced the European Convention on Human Rights into Kosovan law, and expressly stated that the military and the civilian presence would be bound by its standards.

Source: Claire Dyer, The Guardian, 13 November 2006

IRAN: FIXING FACTS AROUND THE POLICY?

'UN inspectors have protested to the US government and a Congressional committee about a report on Iran's nuclear work, calling parts of it "outrageous and dishonest", according to a letter obtained by Reuters in September 2006.

Sent to the head of the House of Representatives' Select Committee on Intelligence by a senior aide to the Director General of the International Atomic Energy Agency, Mohamed ElBaradei, the letter said a committee report dated 23 August contained serious distortions of IAEA findings on Iran's activity.

The letter said the errors suggested Iran's nuclear fuel programme was much more advanced than a series of IAEA reports and Washington's own intelligence assessments have determined. It said the report falsely described Iran to have enriched uranium at its pilot centrifuge plant to weapons-grade level in April, whereas IAEA inspectors had made clear Iran had enriched only to a low level usable for nuclear power reactor fuel. "Furthermore, the IAEA Secretariat takes strong exception to the incorrect and misleading assertion" that the IAEA opted to remove a senior safeguards inspector for supposedly concluding the purpose of Iran's programme was to build weapons, it said. The letter said the congressional report contained "an outrageous and dishonest suggestion" that the inspector was dumped for having not adhered to an alleged IAEA policy barring its "officials from telling the whole truth" about Iran. IAEA spokeswoman Melissa Fleming said: "We felt obliged to put the record straight with regard to the facts on what we have reported on Iran. It's a matter of the integrity of the IAEA."'

Source: Mark Heinrich, Reuters, 14 September 2006

Reviews

Whose Challenge?

Roland McIntosh, *Challenge to Democracy – Politics, Trade Union Power and Economic Failure in the 1970s*, **Politico's Publishing, 400 pages, ISBN 1842751573 £25**

Roland McIntosh was appointed Director General of the National Economic Development Council in 1973. He resigned towards the end of 1977. During the whole of this period he kept a diary in which he recorded his impressions of events, policies and personalities. It was a turbulent period in which the Conservatives lost power following a dispute in the mining industry, to be succeeded by a Labour Government, first under Harold Wilson and then under James Callaghan.

For more than twenty years the diary remained in Ronald McIntosh's possession. In 2003 he showed it to Roy Jenkins, who encouraged him to get it published. Publication took place this year, 2006. The book is a shorter version than the original diary.

Neddy, as it was generally known, was a tripartite organisation, first established in 1962 by the then Prime Minister, Harold MacMillan. Its purpose, as seen by its founder, was to seek cooperation wherever possible on agreed strategies between the government of the day, the employers and unions. It survived not only the Conservative and Labour Governments of the 1960s and 1970s but also the entire period of the Thatcher Government. It was finally abolished by John Major in 1992.

Originally, it was the intention of the Conservative Government to involve employers and unions in joint decisions to curb inflation and promote productivity. There were differences of view within the unions as to whether they should cooperate. The majority were in favour, mainly, to seek, wherever possible, to influence government policies towards economic growth and the improvement of living standards. The opportunity of tripartite consultation, it was felt, should not be refused.

Before his appointment as Director-General of the Council, Ronald McIntosh had held senior positions in the Cabinet Office and the Treasury. He was a top-drawer civil servant with a public school (Charterhouse) and Oxford (Balliol) background. He came with a reputation of competence, liberal views, including support for collective bargaining, and a helpful personality.

The 1970s were difficult years for the British economy. Commodity prices rose sharply, many raw materials more than doubled in price, oil prices rose fourfold and the British balance-of-payments deteriorated. British manufacturing industry had already started on its long-term decline.

The British trade union movement was moving leftwards towards more radical policies. A number of unions, notably the TGWU and the AUEW, had elected left-wing leaders and the miners were in a militant mood to improve their wages and conditions.

At a very early stage in Ronald McIntosh's period at Neddy the Government and the miners came into confrontation. The miners were determined on a much overdue improvement in their pay and conditions. At the height of the crisis the Government rejected an offer by the TUC that the miners should be treated as a special case and that a settlement with them outside the terms of the prevailing incomes policy would not be regarded as a precedent for others. Instead the Government dissolved Parliament and called a General Election on the issue of 'Who Governs Britain?'

The Labour Party won a narrow victory and, with Michael Foot as Secretary of State, the new Government immediately negotiated a settlement with the miners. Ronald McIntosh, to his credit, saw that the Conservative Government had mismanaged the dispute with the miners, but this did not imply that he was in sympathy with the left in the unions or the Labour Party.

His point of view appears to have been that Britain was in deep trouble brought about by the economic losses endured during the Second World War, the loss of the Empire, the low level of investment in British industry, the low level of productivity and growing trade union militancy. Hence, as he saw it, the purpose of the Neddy organisation was to help bring the unions on board for higher productivity and for higher industrial investment. If capitalism and parliamentary democracy were to be saved, cooperation, including necessary concessions, were preferable to confrontation!

Unfortunately, as the book makes clear, he never appears to have shown much appreciation that any active trade unionists and socialists within the Labour Party saw the answers to these problems in different terms but without in any way mounting a 'challenge to democracy'. Indeed, their challenge to mistaken policies was seen by the activists as democracy in action.

Industrial investment was low because those who owned private wealth – industrial tycoons, financiers and bankers – kept it that way. Many of them preferred investment overseas or in property. All the warning signs had been given, for example, in the reports of the industrial working parties set up by Sir Stafford Cripps in the years of the 1945 Labour Government.

Moreover, when Ronald McIntosh quite rightly called for increased investment in industry, he also urged that 'non-productive public expenditure' should be cut. What did he mean by this? Was it the social services and pensions? Why no mention of the high cost of the rearmament programme in post-war Britain, the development of nuclear weapons and the cost of the foreign wars in which Britain has been engaged since 1945?

Ronald McIntosh favoured what he describes as 'consensus policies'. This was to include not only increased investment in industry and a reduction in 'non-productive public expenditure' but also tighter control of the money supply. He thought that taxation and income policies had diminished incentives. Within the area of this 'consensus thinking' he sought to work with the unions and to encourage employers to extend the area of joint regulation of employment conditions. Nevertheless his 'consensus thinking' did not include a commitment to full employment. In May 1977 he wrote, 'that with high unemployment and responsible trade union leadership a return to free collective bargaining need not produce a wage explosion ... '

McIntosh appears to have shared the fear of a number of his contemporaries in power positions that the left in the trade union and labour movement posed a lasting threat. By the left he included not only the familiar names from the unions but also Tony Benn, Michael Foot and Judith Hart. Tony Benn was the member of the Government most actively associated with the effort to promote planning agreements with big firms to ensure that their policies for investments and exports were co-ordinated with the Government's drive for productivity and an improvement in the balance-of-payments. With regard to the election of Labour leader in 1976, McIntosh reveals that if Michael Foot had won he would probably have resigned from the National Economic Development Office.

Ronald McIntosh's favoured union leader during this period was probably Sid Green of the NUR. He speaks of him in very warm terms. He acknowledged a personal liking for some of the more left-wing leaders including Hugh Scanlon and Danny McGarvey. Of Frank Chapple he says that he saw 'everything in terms of the struggle against communism'.

Two of the union leaders who, in my view, emerge with special credit from this book are Jack Jones and Len Murray. Jack Jones never lost his bearings during all the ups and downs of this period. He was always prepared to participate in consultation about economic policy but he never mistook consultation for real economic planning. Effective planning implies that the government of the day has a substantial influence on the control of resources. Economic 'planning' within the Neddy machinery was little more than indicative speculation about the objectives of many different private firms, interested primarily in private profit.

The strength of Len Murray was in his persistence in pointing out that the rigid incomes policy, particularly when enforced by statute, creates more problems than it claims to resolve. In the first place there is the ever-present question about the share of wages in the national income. What of the other constituent elements: profits, interests, rents, pensions, social services and military expenditure? Even within the framework of incomes policy there are never-ending problems about rewards for higher productivity, special payments to attract labour into under-manned occupations, comparability both within an enterprise and with employment elsewhere, equal pay for work of equal value, job evaluation, differentials and problems of very low pay.

McIntosh offers frank observations – not always complimentary – about a number of top civil servants, Conservative politicians and other leading figures. He records that one prominent industrialist said that he would rather go to prison than conform with the provisions in Tony Benn's Industrial Bill about disclosing information to the government and unions. In another passage he describes John Donaldson, the judge at the National Industrial Relations Court, as 'wrongheaded' and whose judgments showed 'little understanding of the contemporary trade union movement'.

The title of this book, *Challenge to Democracy*, invites the question: if there was a challenge from whom and whence did it come? It was not from the labour movement and, in particular, it was not from the unions.

Labour was elected in the 1970s on a programme of economic planning. It was not the unions who resisted effective economic planning: it was the employers. Under Jim Callaghan the Labour Government followed the mistaken policy of imposing a rigid incomes policy on lowly-paid public sector workers.

When, in 1977, Ronald McIntosh indicated that he was going to leave the National Economic Development Office to join the board of a merchant bank, Harry Urwin of the TGWU described it as 'the social security system for top people'.

There are lessons to be learnt from these experiences.

J. E. Mortimer

'24 hours to save the NHS'

Michael Mandelstam, *Betraying the NHS: Health Abandoned*, Jessica Kingsley Publishers, 320 pages, ISBN 1843104822, £14.99

This is an extraordinary book, written by an extraordinary person. The energy and commitment required to research and record this micro-history of health and social care in Suffolk is truly astonishing, and stems from an entirely justifiable sense of outrage. This is communicated in a measured and well-reasoned way, with every assertion supported by documented fact. There is a vast, and easily accessible, reference base. The tragedy, to my mind, is that, in a democracy, and with a Government that, in 1997, famously gave its electorate '24 hours to save the NHS', there should ever have been a need for a book like this.

One of the most depressing aspects of current NHS politics is the mismatch between the glossy guidance documents and the 'corporate tyranny' of the new market in health. 'Listening to local voices' paints a rosy picture of a government that respects the views of its electorate, and yet Primary Care Trusts and Government ministers ignore petitions signed by thousands upon thousands of citizens, and dismiss their concerns as merely 'emotional' or uninformed, insisting that 'less is more'. The genuine despair of patients and clinicians, in the face of attempts to close down service after service, is ignored, because cuts are for their 'own good'. This new NHS recession, which comes at a time of unprecedented investment, seems inexplicable to most people; it is becoming increasingly difficult not to be a conspiracy theorist.

Mandelstam makes the argument that care closer to home, or in patients' homes, should be properly resourced before community hospitals close. Care at home sounds good, as long as it doesn't degenerate into denying hospital care when it is needed. We will still need hospitals, rehabilitation beds, and long-term nursing care for elderly, ill people. The burden of caring for elderly people, with complex medical needs, can be unremitting and exhausting. Weary relatives already witness unseemly battles between social services and primary care trusts over whether care is the financial responsibility of social services or health. The cheapest care, always, is no care at all.

This book stands as a fascinating, if deeply depressing, statement. It also sounds a warning; 'choice', 'modernisation' and 'reform' conceal a privatisation agenda which is being carried out with haste and deceit. By the next election, the NHS will have ceased to exist, as large private companies roll in to take over primary care and the lucrative NHS commissioning budgets. This is going unnoticed for the same reason that Shipman went unnoticed; people simply don't believe it is possible. The implications are not just in the realms of health; whole communities feel disenfranchised and apathetic about the political process and this is dangerous for democracy. People in power do not like democracy, and apathy is a strong tool for those who would abuse it. I wish that every MP (not just New Labour) would read this book and reflect on its message.

Asked how long he thought the NHS would last, Bevan replied: 'as long as there are people left to defend it'. Mandelstam recognises that health care is complex, and he cannot offer solutions. However, his whole book is an impassioned defence of an NHS that could be honest, transparent, participative, and equitable.

Elizabeth Barrett

Washington Dysfunctional

Christopher Meyer, *DC Confidential: The Controversial Memoirs of Britain's Ambassador at the Time of 9/11 and the Run-up to the Iraq War*, Phoenix, 344 pages, paperback ISBN 0753821303 £8.99

Christopher Meyer's reminiscences of his time as ambassador to Washington, long considered the top posting in the diplomatic service, do provide an insight for outsiders to this strange world of stiff protocol, friendships that are only such due to their utility, and spooks. His book is also revealing of the dreadfully dysfunctional state administration that was Britain under Blair. Certainly, if the other departments of state in Whitehall were operating as the Foreign Office was then, it goes a long way to helping us understand why the Home Office is 'unfit for purpose', and delivery of policies has been so difficult for New Labour.

DC Confidential does give us a behind-the-doors glimpse of diplomacy at its most pedantic. Who should sit beside whom at the grand dinners? Should the Ambassador's wife accompany him to certain functions, and should he be so annoyed when an invitation for his spouse is not forthcoming? Why should he be worrying his little head about redecorating of the British Embassy, 'The Great House', when there's a bloody war going on in Kosovo?

Ah, Kosovo! A topic of substance, and what is to be the first substantial test for Blair's doctrine of the international community. This is the militarist doctrine espoused by him at a meeting of the Economic Club in Chicago. Meyer's account of the behind the scenes action is to some degree revealing. External affairs in the United Kingdom appear to have been the subject of a by-pass operation. The years of experience accumulated by our Foreign Office were no longer needed. Downing Street was in control. It was as though Tony Blair, sidelined from economic and budgetary policy by Gordon Brown, had to find something to make him famous, so leapt on foreign affairs like a little boy getting a cowboy outfit.

The arrogance of the upstarts was revealed during the period of Blair's visit to the United States in April 1999. He took it upon himself to preach to the Americans on the need to have a credible ground force threat to Milosovic for the bombing of Yugoslavia to be successful. But, worse than that, Clinton went ballistic as he suspected Alastair Campbell of briefing against him. Also annoying to Clinton was the assumption of some sort of equality between a British prime minister and an American president. Remember the question, 'how many battalions does the Pope have?' Then ask the question 'what was Britain's contribution to the Kosovo bombing?', and the answer is 48 aircraft to the American's 1,152.

Lesson one, therefore, is if you're going to crawl to an American president, don't annoy him first. But another lesson was learned from that conflagration. It is that you can lie in your propaganda regarding far-off foreign parts in a way that you cannot at home. Wagging the dog thus became a mainstream policy tool, but it only succeeds if the objective is reached quickly. The interventions in Afghanistan and then Iraq should all have been over by now but they're not. Indeed, the mission is still not accomplished in Kosovo.

The revelation of the fabrication of the case for war from the ambassador's point of view is interesting to a student of this period; unfortunately for Christopher Meyer, we now have evidence that refutes most of the arguments that led him to conclude that these wars were in someway justified. His reference to the Iraqi's weapons of mass destruction report being 'defective and mendacious' ignores the fact the United States removed 8,000 pages from the 11,000 page report before the United Nations had full view of it (see *Spokesman 77, 78 &81*). His memory of the Kosovo bombing omits the contemporary accounts that report mass evacuation as happening after the bombing started, and therefore it could not have been the reason to start bombing.

Meyer's account is still valuable as it exposes some possible reasons for the failure of foreign policy which will surely become the Blair Legacy. A powerful press officer recruited from the British tabloids, whose motto is never to let the facts get in the way of a good story, may have been able to provide mendacious jingoism to accompany the drums of war. But, as is now revealed, he can contribute nothing to the complexity of rebuilding the broken lives and ruined homes that are always the result of choosing war as a foreign policy option.

I mused by the way at an autobiographical passage where Meyer made reference to a post-graduate year he spent at the School of Advanced International

Studies in Bologna, later to be called the Paul H. Nitze School. For any student of international politics, Nitze's name should be enough to tell you what territory you are in, but not, it appears, our future ambassador to the US of A. In his own words, he later discovered from a Soviet diplomat that the school was funded by the CIA. What do they teach them at Cambridge? Nitze was the arch cold warrior of the United States, a friend and promoter of the views of Edward Teller. He could almost be described as Dr Strangelove's apprentice.

Henry McCubbin

Mao

Yves Chevrier, *Mao and the Chinese Revolution*, Interlink Books, 158 pages, Northampton, Mass. ISBN 1566565146 $15

Jung Chang and Jon Halliday, *Mao: The Unknown Story*, 814 pages, Vintage Books, ISBN 0099461552 £15

Roderick MacFarquhar and Michael Schoenhals, *Mao's Last Revolution*, The Belknap Press of Harvard University Press, 693 pages, ISBN 0674023323 £22.95

Jung Chang is the best selling author of *Wild Swans*, who began her education as a Red Guard when she was fourteen years old, and took up a variety of occupations ('barefoot doctor', steelworker, electrician) before becoming a student of English at Sichuan University. She came to Britain in 1978, and subsequently gained a PhD in Linguistics at York.

Jon Halliday was an established author before he met his colleague.

Evidently the tribulations undergone by Jung Chang, so harrowingly described in *Wild Swans*, have not disposed her to seek to prettify the biography of Mao. He is presented as having direct responsibility for the deaths of seventy million Chinese, and his strenuous politicking throughout a tumultuous life is invariably seen through the eyes of his factional opponents. Evidently these people must have sometimes been right, perhaps even often right. But it would be contrary to everything we know to assume that this was always so. When the first edition was published, it received extraordinary acclaim, and was celebrated all the way across the press, giving rise to the characterisation of Mao as 'the greatest monster of them all'. But this is unlikely to be the last word, not least because of its free approach to the evidence.

Roderick MacFarquhar and Michael Schoenhals embarked upon their history of the Cultural Revolution with no greater enthusiasm for the merits of its progenitor. But their very large book is more compelling, not because it plays down atrocities committed by Mao or on his instructions, but because it is unwilling to speculate about his motives or to enter into imaginative reconstructions of the events it chronicles.

Yves Chevrier has given us a little book on Mao's Revolutions, which characterises their architect as 'both tyrant and perpetual rebel', 'the father of the tragic utopia that was Maoism'.

'Mao's unique position', he says, 'comes from combining three exceptional qualities as revolutionary, empire builder and totalitarian dictator'. But the strength of this little book lies in its readiness to follow the arguments of Mao's adversaries, from Chen Duxiu to Liu Shaoqi or Wang Ming. This gives his work some real credibility.

James Holt

The Vegetarians' Case Book

Tristram Stuart, *The Bloodless Revolution: Radical Vegetarians and the Discovery of India*, **HarperCollins, 628 pages, hardback ISBN0007128924 £25**

I was brought up in a Quaker family, where many of my parents' Quaker friends were vegetarians. As a child it seemed to me that they were a bit odd, with their beards, open neck collars, sandals and their luggage in a rucksack. I realised later that their vegetarianism was part of their pacifism and general repugnance to all forms of violence, feelings which I certainly shared with my parents. Edward Carpenter was at one time my democratic socialist hero, but I never became a vegetarian. Although I could not eat rabbit, once having kept rabbits, and have never liked red meat, I just hoped that there were more humane ways of killing. The only logical case for protecting animals from killing seemed to me to be that of the vegans, because I did not see what was to happen to the male offspring of the cows or ewes if only the females were to be kept for their milk, and I liked all dairy products too much to give them up. I am also very fond of fish and have taught myself not to mind catching them and boiling crabs and lobsters.

What I had no idea of until I read Tristram Stuart's monumental and beautiful book was the roll of honour of the vegetarians running from Pythagoras, Socrates and Diogenes to Bernard Shaw and including Voltaire and Rousseau, Bacon, Descartes and Newton, Franklin, Shelley and Thoreau, Gandhi and – heaven forfend! – Hitler. Nor had I any idea of the controversies about meat eating and animal and human rights inside Christian orthodoxy and among the French revolutionaries, nor of the widespread influence of Indian thought on the diets of early British imperialists. Christians went back to the Bible and saw in the story of the Garden of Eden and the lamb lying down with the lion the justification for a prelapsarian heritage, which human population increase had rendered extinct. For non-Christians the association of meat eating and human violence is one of the continuing themes uniting all vegetarians, with the Brahmins and Buddhists providing the best evidence for vegetarian pacifism. Vegetarians in the past, according to Tristram Stuart, had varied reasons for their conviction, but the subtitle to his book indicates that what most of them seem to have had in common was their admiration for the longevity of Indian vegetarians as compared with Europeans. Medical science seems to have narrowed the difference, so that I am not so impressed with this argument.

A central part of the argument against vegetarianism in the past was concerned with the Darwinian theory of evolution. If survival of the fittest in changing climatic conditions on the planet is how the great variety of species is explained and how the human species has evolved, this must have meant the killing off of the less fit. We are all what we are, whether we like it or not, the result of an immensely long process of elimination. The population of any species, moreover, would grow far beyond its capacity to survive if it were not for the action of predators. The culling of human beings in wars may have been necessary for human survival, and may, as some believe, still be necessary as population growth exceeds the resources available. This was the argument of Thomas Malthus, based on Buffon's principle that death was the mother of life, which challenged all those like Shelley and Godwin who believed that a more egalitarian society based on vegetarian principles would survive.

By far the most impressive case for a mainly vegetable human diet was and still is today the ecological one, that grazing animals use many times (some have claimed ten times) the amount of land for a given quantity of human food. Adam Smith among others recognised this. Enclosures and the Highland Clearances for sheep grazing not only destroyed the poor man's commons, but reduced the productivity of the land for increasing populations. Today, moreover, the demand for beef production is leading to the destruction of millions of acres of tropical forest cover which is essential for the self-regulation of the planet's climate. Few people are likely to become vegetarians, let alone vegans, as a result of such considerations, but more and more are likely to reduce the amount of meat in their diet. It is an important lesson of this book that most of those in the past who advocated a vegetarian diet allowed for a small proportion of animal products in their meals. Jamie Oliver's war on beef burgers in school meals does not imply, as the cartoonists suggest, a regime of 'rabbit food' in their place. Human teeth and digestive systems are quite capable of dealing with both vegetables and meat in moderation to ensure a healthy diet. *Carpe diem!*

Michael Barratt Brown